simply
baking

Simply
baking

100 fuss-free recipes for everyday cooking

Bath · New York · Cologne · Melbourne · Delhi
Hong Kong · Shenzhen · Singapore

This edition published by Parragon Books Ltd in 2016

Parragon Books Ltd
Chartist House
15–17 Trim Street
Bath BA1 1HA, UK
www.parragon.com

Copyright © Parragon Books Ltd 2011–2016

Introduction by Linda Doeser
New recipes by Sandra Baddeley
Additional photography by Mike Cooper
Additional food styling by Sumi Glass

ISBN: 978-1-4748-5053-7

Printed in China

Notes for the Reader
This book uses both metric and imperial measurements. Follow the same units of measurement throughout; do not mix metric and imperial. All spoon measurements are level: teaspoons are assumed to be 5 ml, and tablespoons are assumed to be 15 ml. Unless otherwise stated, milk is assumed to be full fat, eggs and individual fruits and vegetables are medium, pepper is freshly ground black pepper and salt is table salt. Unless otherwise stated, all root vegetables should be peeled prior to using.

The times given are an approximate guide only. Preparation times differ according to the techniques used by different people and the cooking times may also vary from those given.

Recipes using raw or very lightly cooked eggs should be avoided by infants, the elderly, pregnant women, convalescents and anyone suffering from an illness. Pregnant and breastfeeding women are advised to avoid eating peanuts and peanut products. Sufferers from nut allergies should be aware that some of the ready-made ingredients used in the recipes in this book may contain nuts. Always check the packaging before use.

Bundt ® is a registered trade mark of Northland Aluminium Products, Inc.

The publisher would like to thank the following for permission to reproduce copyright material on the front cover: Chocolate cake on a plate © Ray Kachatorian/Getty Images.

Contents

Introduction

There is something extraordinarily satisfying about baking. It's partly the sheer magic of taking a few simple ingredients – flour, butter, sugar, eggs and some dried fruit or chocolate chips, for example – and turning them into a luscious family cake, a batch of tasty chewy flapjacks or a tempting pile of biscuits.

It's also the warm sense of approval that you receive from family and friends when you offer them home-baked muffins with a cup of tea or a slice of creamy cheesecake at the end of a meal, knowing that their enjoyment is far greater than the effort of making these treats. In fact, baking is probably the most rewarding and instantly gratifying type of all cooking.

There is a widespread belief that baking is tricky and requires special skills, but nothing could be further from the truth. Of course, elaborately layered gateaux or fragile pastry confections are probably best left to the more experienced or professional cook, but even a novice can rustle up a perfect batch of brownies, a delicious drizzle cake, a dozen crisp cookies or an elegant torte for dessert.

In baking, it is not essential to have a special talent and there's no secret knack – just carefully measure each ingredient and work steadily through each step of the process and success is guaranteed.

Family cakes are for everyday eating, but this doesn't mean that they have to be dull. They may be flavoured with fresh or dried fruit, spices, chocolate, nuts or honey and can be decorated with simple icings or sprinkled with sugar, nuts or other tasty toppings.

Those who are new to home baking might want to start with slices and bars. These are virtually foolproof, not least because cutting them to shape after cooking ensures that they always look neat and professional. They are perfect for an after-school snack and ideal as a pick-me-up after a busy day – many are packed with energy and not too sugary.

Small cakes and cookies are simplicity itself and are a great way for parents or grandparents to introduce small children to the delights of home baking.

Finally, there is a chapter of beautiful and luxurious desserts, some traditional and others contemporary – all of them impressive and yet easy to bake.

Top Tips for Success

• Always read through the recipe before you start and collect together all the ingredients and equipment that you will need.

• Remove ingredients normally stored in the refrigerator about 30 minutes beforehand so that they can come to room temperature. This is especially important with eggs as if they are very cold, they may curdle.

• Accurate measurement of the ingredients is more important with baking than with virtually any other kind of cooking. Weigh dry ingredients on reliable scales. Spoon measurements should be levelled off with the blade of a knife. Do not pour small quantities of liquid, such as vanilla extract, into a measuring spoon held over the mixing bowl to avoid over-filling and so spoiling the flavour of your baking. The jug for measuring liquids should stand on a flat surface and you should check the measure at eye level.

• Always use the size and shape of cake tin specified in the recipe. A tin that is too large will result in cracks and airholes, while one that is too small is likely to cause the cake to burn or the mixture to overflow, with uneven and disappointing results.

• Always preheat the oven to the specified temperature. An oven that is not hot enough will cause cakes to sink, while one that is too hot will make them crack. Avoid opening the oven, especially if you are baking a cake that needs to rise. If you cannot resist taking a peek, wait until at least halfway through the cooking time.

• Do not leave the mixture standing for any length of time after mixing, unless the recipe specifies. If you are using self-raising flour and/ or baking powder, the raising agent begins to work as soon as liquid is added. Delay in putting the cake in the oven may prevent it from rising.

• A good way to toast nuts and avoid the risk of scorching them is to spread them out – about 4 tablespoons at a time – on a microwave-safe plate and microwave on high for 15–20 seconds.

• Chocolate can also be melted in the microwave. Break the chocolate into pieces and put into a microwave-safe bowl. Heat on medium for 10 seconds, then stir. Heat for another 10 seconds and stir again. Continue this process until all the chocolate has melted. Melt white chocolate on a low rather than medium heat. Otherwise, put the chocolate into a heatproof bowl set over a pan of barely simmering water until melted.

1

Family
Cakes

chocolate fudge cake

SERVES 8

175 g/6 oz unsalted butter, softened, plus extra for greasing

175 g/6 oz golden caster sugar

3 eggs, beaten

3 tbsp golden syrup

40 g/1½ oz ground almonds

175 g/6 oz self-raising flour

pinch of salt

40 g/1½ oz cocoa powder

icing

225 g/8 oz plain chocolate, broken into pieces

55 g/2 oz dark muscovado sugar

225 g/8 oz unsalted butter, diced

5 tbsp evaporated milk

½ tsp vanilla extract

1 Grease two 20-cm/8-inch sandwich tins and line the bases with baking paper.

2 To make the icing, place the chocolate, muscovado sugar, diced butter, evaporated milk and vanilla extract in a heavy-based saucepan. Heat gently, stirring constantly, until melted. Pour into a bowl and leave to cool. Cover and chill in the refrigerator for 1 hour, or until spreadable.

3 Preheat the oven to 180°C/350°F/Gas Mark 4. Place the butter and caster sugar in a bowl and beat together until light and fluffy. Gradually beat in the eggs. Stir in the golden syrup and ground almonds. Sift the flour, salt and cocoa powder into a separate bowl, then fold into the mixture. Add a little water, if necessary, to make a dropping consistency.

4 Spoon the mixture into the prepared tins and bake in the preheated oven for 30–35 minutes, or until springy to the touch and a skewer inserted into the centre comes out clean.

5 Leave the cakes in the tins for 5 minutes, then turn out onto wire racks to cool completely. When the cakes are cold, sandwich them together with half the icing. Spread the remaining icing over the top and sides of the cake.

carrot & ginger cake

SERVES 10

butter, for greasing

280 g/10 oz plain flour

1 tsp baking powder

1 tsp bicarbonate of soda

2 tsp ground ginger

½ tsp salt

175 g/6 oz dark muscovado sugar

325 g/11½ oz grated carrots

2 pieces chopped stem ginger

1 tbsp grated fresh ginger

55 g/2 oz raisins

2 eggs, beaten

3 tbsp sunflower oil

juice of 1 orange

strips of orange zest, to decorate

icing

225 g/8 oz cream cheese

4 tbsp icing sugar

1 tsp vanilla extract

1 Preheat the oven to 180°C/350°F/Gas Mark 4. Grease a 20-cm/8-inch round cake tin and line with baking paper.

2 Sift the flour, baking powder, bicarbonate of soda, ground ginger and salt into a bowl. Stir in the muscovado sugar, carrots, stem ginger, fresh ginger and raisins. Beat together the eggs, oil and orange juice, then pour into the bowl with the dry ingredients. Mix together well.

3 Spoon the mixture into the prepared tin and bake in the preheated oven for 1–1¼ hours, until firm to the touch and a skewer inserted into the centre of the cake comes out clean. Leave to cool in the tin.

4 To make the icing, place the cream cheese in a bowl and beat to soften. Sift in the icing sugar and add the vanilla extract. Mix well.

5 Remove the cake from the tin and spread the icing over the top. Decorate the cake with strips of orange zest and serve.

victoria sponge cake

SERVES 8–10

175 g/6 oz butter, softened, plus extra for greasing

175 g/6 oz caster sugar

3 eggs, beaten

175 g/6 oz self-raising flour

pinch of salt

3 tbsp raspberry jam

1 tbsp caster or icing sugar

1 Preheat the oven to 180°C/350°F/Gas Mark 4. Grease two 20-cm/8-inch sandwich tins and line with baking paper.

2 Cream the butter and caster sugar together in a mixing bowl using a wooden spoon or a hand-held mixer until the mixture is pale in colour and light and fluffy. Add the eggs a little at a time, beating well after each addition. Sift the flour and salt and carefully add to the mixture, folding it in with a metal spoon or a spatula.

3 Spoon the mixture into the prepared tins and smooth over with the spatula.

4 Place them on the same shelf in the centre of the preheated oven and bake for 25–30 minutes, until well risen, golden brown and beginning to shrink from the sides of the tin.

5 Remove from the oven and allow to cool slightly. Loosen the cakes from around the edge of the tins using a palette knife. Turn the cakes out onto a clean tea towel, remove the paper and invert them onto a wire rack. When completely cool, sandwich the cakes together with the jam and sprinkle the top with the caster or icing sugar.

red velvet cake

SERVES 12

225 g/8 oz unsalted butter, plus extra for greasing

4 tbsp water

55 g/2 oz cocoa powder

3 eggs

250 ml/9 fl oz buttermilk

2 tsp vanilla extract

2 tbsp red edible food colouring

280 g/10 oz plain flour

55 g/2 oz cornflour

1½ tsp baking powder

280 g/10 oz caster sugar

frosting

250 g/9 oz cream cheese

40 g/1½ oz unsalted butter

3 tbsp caster sugar

1 tsp vanilla extract

1 Preheat the oven to 190°C/375°F/Gas Mark 5. Grease two 23-cm/9-inch sandwich tins and line with baking paper.

2 Place the butter, water and cocoa powder in a small saucepan and heat gently, without boiling, stirring until melted and smooth. Remove from the heat and leave to cool slightly. Beat together the eggs, buttermilk, vanilla extract and food colouring until frothy. Beat in the butter mixture. Sift together the flour, cornflour and baking powder, then stir quickly and evenly into the mixture with the caster sugar.

3 Spoon the mixture into the prepared tins and bake in the preheated oven for 25–30 minutes, or until risen and firm to the touch. Leave to cool in the tins for 3–4 minutes, then turn out onto a wire rack to cool completely.

4 To make the frosting, beat together all the ingredients until smooth. Use about half of the frosting to sandwich the cakes together, then spread the remainder over the top, swirling with a palette knife.

marble cake

SERVES 10

55 g/2 oz plain chocolate

1 tbsp strong black coffee

280 g/10 oz self-raising flour

1 tsp baking powder

225 g/8 oz butter, softened, plus extra for greasing

225 g/8 oz golden caster sugar

4 eggs, beaten

50 g/1¾ oz ground almonds

2 tbsp milk

1 tsp vanilla extract

icing

125 g/4½ oz plain chocolate

2 tbsp butter

2 tbsp water

1 Preheat the oven to 180°C/350°F/Gas Mark 4. Grease a 1.7-litre/3-pint ring mould.

2 Put the chocolate and coffee in a heatproof bowl set over a saucepan of gently simmering water. Heat until melted. Leave to cool.

3 Sift the flour and baking powder into a bowl. Add the butter, sugar, eggs, ground almonds and milk. Beat well until smooth.

4 Transfer half of the mixture to a separate bowl and stir in the vanilla extract. Stir the cooled chocolate mixture into the other half of the mixture. Place spoonfuls of the two mixtures alternately into the prepared ring mould, then drag a skewer through to create a marbled effect. Smooth the top.

5 Bake in the preheated oven for 50–60 minutes, until risen and a skewer inserted into the centre comes out clean. Leave in the mould for 5 minutes, then turn out onto a wire rack to cool.

6 To make the icing, put the chocolate, butter and water into a heatproof bowl set over a saucepan of gently simmering water. Heat until melted. Stir and pour over the cake, working quickly to coat the top and sides. Leave to set before serving.

gingerbread

SERVES 12–16

450 g/1 lb plain flour

1 tbsp baking powder

1 tsp bicarbonate of soda

1 tbsp ground ginger

175 g/6 oz unsalted butter, plus extra for greasing

175 g/6 oz soft dark brown sugar

175 g/6 oz black treacle

175 g/6 oz golden syrup

1 egg, beaten

300 ml/10 fl oz milk

1 Preheat the oven to 160°C/325°F/Gas Mark 3. Grease a 23-cm/9-inch square cake tin and line with baking paper.

2 Sift together the flour, baking powder, bicarbonate of soda and ground ginger into a large mixing bowl. Place the butter, sugar, treacle and golden syrup in a medium saucepan and heat over a low heat until the butter has melted and the sugar has dissolved. Allow to cool slightly.

3 Mix the egg with the milk and add to the cooled butter mixture. Add all the liquid ingredients to the flour mixture and beat well using a wooden spoon until the mixture is smooth and glossy.

4 Spoon the mixture into the prepared tin and bake in the centre of the preheated oven for 1½ hours, until well risen and just firm to the touch. This gives a lovely sticky gingerbread, but if you like a firmer cake cook for a further 15 minutes.

5 Remove from the oven and allow the cake to cool in the tin. When cool, remove the cake from the tin.

honey & almond cake

SERVES 8

75 g/2¾ oz soft margarine, plus extra for greasing

75 g/2¾ oz soft light brown sugar

2 eggs

175 g/6 oz self-raising flour

1 tsp baking powder

4 tbsp milk

2 tbsp clear honey

50 g/1¾ oz flaked almonds

syrup

225 g/8 oz honey

2 tbsp lemon juice

1 Preheat the oven to 180°C/350°F/Gas Mark 4. Grease an 18-cm/7-inch round cake tin and line with baking paper.

2 Place the margarine, sugar, eggs, flour, baking powder, milk and honey in a large mixing bowl and beat well with a wooden spoon for about 1 minute, or until all of the ingredients are thoroughly combined.

3 Spoon into the prepared tin, smooth the surface with the back of a spoon or a knife and sprinkle with the almonds. Bake in the preheated oven for about 50 minutes, or until well risen and a skewer inserted into the centre comes out clean.

4 Meanwhile, make the syrup. Combine the honey and lemon juice in a small saucepan and simmer over a low heat for about 5 minutes, or until the syrup coats the back of a spoon.

5 As soon as the cake comes out of the oven, pour the syrup over it, letting it soak into the cake. Leave the cake to cool in the tin for at least 2 hours before slicing.

date & walnut loaf

SERVES 8

100 g/3½ oz dates, stoned and chopped

½ tsp bicarbonate of soda

finely grated rind of ½ lemon

100 ml/3½ fl oz hot tea

40 g/1½ oz unsalted butter, plus extra for greasing

70 g/2½ oz light muscovado sugar

1 small egg

125 g/4½ oz self-raising flour

25 g/1 oz walnuts, chopped

walnut halves, to decorate

1 Preheat the oven to 180°C/350°F/Gas Mark 4. Grease a 450-g/1-lb loaf tin and line with baking paper.

2 Place the dates, bicarbonate of soda and lemon rind in a bowl and add the hot tea. Leave to soak for 10 minutes until softened.

3 Cream the butter and sugar together until light and fluffy, then beat in the egg. Stir in the date mixture.

4 Fold in the flour using a large metal spoon, then fold in the walnuts. Spoon the mixture into the prepared cake tin and smooth the surface. Top with the walnut halves.

5 Bake in the preheated oven for 35–40 minutes or until risen, firm and golden brown. Cool for 10 minutes in the tin, then turn out onto a wire rack to cool completely.

blueberry & lemon drizzle cake

SERVES 9

225 g/8 oz butter, softened, plus extra for greasing

225 g/8 oz golden caster sugar

4 eggs, beaten

250 g/9 oz self-raising flour, sifted

finely grated rind of 1 lemon

25 g/1 oz ground almonds

juice of 1 lemon

200 g/7 oz fresh blueberries

topping

juice of 2 lemons

115 g/4 oz golden caster sugar

55 g/2 oz icing sugar

1 Preheat the oven to 180°C/350°F/Gas Mark 4. Grease a 20-cm/8-inch square cake tin and line with baking paper.

2 Put the butter and caster sugar in a bowl and beat together until light and fluffy. Gradually beat in the eggs, adding a little flour towards the end to prevent curdling. Beat in the lemon rind, then fold in the remaining flour and the almonds with enough lemon juice to make a dropping consistency.

3 Fold in three quarters of the blueberries and spoon into the prepared tin. Smooth the surface, then scatter the remaining blueberries on top. Bake in the preheated oven for about 1 hour, until firm to the touch and a skewer inserted into the centre comes out clean.

4 Meanwhile, make the topping. Put the lemon juice and caster sugar into a bowl and mix together. As soon as the cake comes out of the oven, prick it all over with a fine skewer and pour over the lemon mixture. Mix the icing sugar with a little water and drizzle over the cake. Leave in the tin until completely cool, then cut into squares.

chocolate & walnut cake

4 eggs

125 g/4½ oz caster sugar

75 g/2¾ oz plain chocolate, broken into pieces

125 g/4½ oz plain flour

1 tbsp cocoa powder

2 tbsp butter, melted, plus extra for greasing

115 g/4 oz finely chopped walnuts

walnut halves, to decorate

icing

75 g/2¾ oz plain chocolate

115 g/4 oz butter

175 g/6 oz icing sugar

2 tbsp milk

1 Preheat the oven to 160°C/325°F/Gas Mark 3. Grease an 18-cm/7-inch deep round cake tin and line with baking paper.

2 Place the eggs and caster sugar in a bowl and whisk with an electric hand-held whisk for 10 minutes, or until foamy and a trail is left when the whisk is dragged across the surface. Put the chocolate in a heatproof bowl set over a saucepan of gently simmering water until melted.

3 Sift the flour and cocoa together and fold into the egg and sugar mixture with a spoon or a palette knife. Fold in the melted butter, melted chocolate and chopped walnuts. Spoon into the prepared tin and bake in the preheated oven for 30–35 minutes, or until springy to the touch.

4 Leave to cool in the tin for 5 minutes, then transfer to a wire rack and leave to cool completely.

5 To make the icing, melt the chocolate as above and leave to cool slightly. Beat together the butter, icing sugar and milk until the mixture is pale and fluffy. Whisk in the melted chocolate.

6 Cut the cake into two layers of equal thickness. Place the bottom half on a serving plate, spread with some of the icing and put the other half on top. Spread the remaining icing over the top of the cake with a palette knife. Decorate with walnut halves and serve.

jewel-topped madeira cake

SERVES 8–10

225 g/8 oz butter, softened, plus extra for greasing

225 g/8 oz golden caster sugar

finely grated rind of 1 lemon

4 eggs, beaten

350 g/12 oz self-raising flour, sifted

2–3 tbsp milk

fruit topping

2½ tbsp honey

300 g/10½ oz glacé fruit, sliced

1 Preheat the oven to 160°C/325°F/Gas Mark 3. Grease a 20-cm/8-inch deep round cake tin and line with baking paper.

2 Put the butter, sugar and lemon rind in a bowl and beat together until light and fluffy. Gradually beat in the eggs. Gently fold in the flour, adding enough milk to make a soft dropping consistency.

3 Spoon the mixture into the prepared tin and bake in the preheated oven for 1½–1¾ hours, until risen and golden and a skewer inserted into the centre comes out clean.

4 Leave in the tin for 10 minutes, then turn out, remove the paper and place on a wire rack to cool. To make the topping, brush the honey over the cake and arrange the fruit on top.

pineapple & coconut ring cake

SERVES 12

432 g/15½ oz canned pineapple rings, drained

115 g/4 oz unsalted butter, softened, plus extra for greasing

175 g/6 oz caster sugar

2 eggs and 1 egg yolk, beaten together

225 g/8 oz plain flour

1 tsp baking powder

½ tsp bicarbonate of soda

40 g/1½ oz desiccated coconut

frosting

175 g/6 oz cream cheese

175 g/6 oz icing sugar

1 Preheat the oven to 180°C/350°F/Gas Mark 4. Grease a 24-cm/9½-inch ring mould. Place the pineapple rings in a blender or food processor and process briefly until just crushed.

2 Beat together the butter and caster sugar until light and fluffy. Gradually beat in the egg until combined. Sift together the flour, baking powder and bicarbonate of soda over the egg mixture and fold in. Then fold in the crushed pineapple and the coconut.

3 Spoon the mixture into the prepared tin and bake in the preheated oven for 25 minutes, until a skewer inserted into the centre comes out clean.

4 Allow to cool in the tin for 10 minutes before turning out onto a wire rack to cool.

5 To make the frosting, mix together the cream cheese and icing sugar and spread over the cooled cake.

coffee streusel cake

SERVES 8–10

225 g/8 oz plain flour

1 tbsp baking powder

70 g/2½ oz caster sugar

150 ml/5 fl oz milk

2 eggs

115 g/4 oz butter, melted and cooled, plus extra for greasing

2 tbsp instant coffee granules, dissolved in 1 tbsp boiling water

50 g/1¾ oz chopped almonds

icing sugar, for dusting

topping

70 g/2½ oz self-raising flour

70 g/2½ oz demerara sugar

2 tbsp butter, cut into small pieces

1 tsp ground mixed spice

1 tbsp water

1 Preheat the oven to 190°C/375°F/Gas Mark 5. Grease a 23-cm/9-inch loose-based round cake tin and line with baking paper.

2 Sift the plain flour and baking powder into a mixing bowl, then stir in the caster sugar.

3 Whisk the milk, eggs, melted butter and coffee mixture together and pour onto the dry ingredients. Add the chopped almonds and mix lightly together. Spoon the mixture into the prepared tin.

4 To make the topping, mix the self-raising flour and demerara sugar together in a bowl. Rub in the butter with your fingertips until the mixture resembles breadcrumbs. Sprinkle in the mixed spice and add the water and bring the mixture together in loose crumbs. Sprinkle the topping evenly over the cake.

5 Bake in the preheated oven for 50 minutes to 1 hour. Cover loosely with foil if the topping starts to brown too quickly.

6 Leave to cool in the tin. Remove the cake from the tin and dust with icing sugar just before serving.

honey spice cake

SERVES 8–10

**150 g/5½ oz butter,
plus extra for greasing**

**175 g/6 oz light muscovado
sugar**

250 g/9 oz honey

1 tbsp water

225 g/8 oz self-raising flour

½ tsp ground ginger

½ tsp ground cinnamon

½ tsp caraway seeds

**seeds from 8 cardamom
pods, ground**

2 eggs, beaten

icing

280 g/10 oz icing sugar

1 Preheat the oven to 180°C/350°F/Gas Mark 4. Grease a 23-cm/9-inch round cake tin and line with baking paper.

2 Put the butter, muscovado sugar, honey and water into a saucepan. Heat gently until the butter has melted and the sugar has dissolved. Remove from the heat and leave to cool for 10 minutes.

3 Sift the flour into a bowl and mix in the ginger, cinnamon, caraway seeds and cardamom seeds. Make a well in the centre, pour in the honey mixture and the eggs, and beat well until smooth.

4 Spoon the mixture into the prepared tin and bake in the preheated oven for 40–50 minutes, until well risen and a skewer inserted into the centre comes out clean. Leave in the tin for 5 minutes, then turn out onto a wire rack to cool.

5 To make the icing, sift the icing sugar into a bowl. Stir in enough warm water to make a smooth, flowing icing. Spoon over the cake, letting it flow down the sides. Leave to set before serving.

upside-down apple cake

SERVES 6–8

700 g/1 lb 9 oz cooking apples

8 cloves

250 g/9 oz caster sugar

140 g/5 oz butter, plus extra for greasing

2 eggs

25 g/1 oz flaked almonds, lightly toasted

25 g/1 oz hazelnuts, lightly toasted and ground

125 ml/4 fl oz double cream

125 ml/4 fl oz milk

½ tsp ground mixed spice

150 g/5½ oz self-raising flour, sifted

whipped cream, to serve

1 Preheat the oven to 180°C/350°F/Gas Mark 4. Grease a 20-cm/8-inch round cake tin.

2 Bring a large saucepan of water to the boil. Peel and core the apples, cut into slices, then add them to the pan with the cloves. Lower the heat and simmer for 5 minutes, then remove from the heat. Drain well. Discard the cloves. Leave the apples to cool a little.

3 Arrange the cooked apple slices over the bottom of the prepared tin and sprinkle over 2 tablespoons of the sugar.

4 In a separate bowl, cream the butter and the remaining sugar together. Gradually mix in the eggs, then the nuts, cream, milk and mixed spice. Gradually beat in the flour until smooth. Spread the mixture evenly over the apples, then bake in the preheated oven for about 40 minutes, until golden and a skewer inserted into the centre comes out clean.

5 Remove from the oven and leave to cool in the tin for 5 minutes, then turn out onto a serving plate. Serve hot with whipped cream.

chocolate orange ring cake

SERVES 8–10

2 small oranges

85 g/3 oz plain chocolate

250 g/9 oz self-raising flour

1½ tsp baking powder

175 g/6 oz butter, softened, plus extra for greasing

200 g/7 oz caster sugar

3 eggs, beaten

topping

175 g/6 oz icing sugar

2 tbsp orange juice

55 g/2 oz plain chocolate, broken into pieces

1 Preheat the oven to 160°C/325°F/Gas Mark 3. Grease an 850-ml/1½-pint ring mould. Grate the rind from one of the oranges and set aside. Pare the rind from the other orange and set aside. Cut the skin and pith from the oranges, then cut them into segments by cutting down between the membranes with a sharp knife. Chop the segments into small pieces, reserving as much juice as possible. Grate the chocolate coarsely.

2 Sift the flour and baking powder into a bowl. Add the butter, caster sugar, eggs, grated orange rind and any reserved juice. Beat until the mixture is smooth. Fold in the chopped oranges and grated chocolate. Spoon the mixture into the prepared tin and bake in the preheated oven for 40 minutes, or until well risen and golden brown. Leave in the tin for 5 minutes, then turn out onto a wire rack to cool.

3 Sift the icing sugar into a bowl and stir in enough orange juice to make a coating consistency. Drizzle the icing over the cake. Put the chocolate in a heatproof bowl set over a saucepan of gently simmering water until melted. Drizzle the melted chocolate over the cake. Cut the reserved pared orange rind into thin strips and scatter over the cake.

cherry & almond cake

SERVES 8

300 g/10½ oz glacé cherries

175 g/6 oz butter, softened, plus extra for greasing

175 g/6 oz golden caster sugar

3 eggs

40 g/1½ oz ground almonds

280 g/10 oz plain flour

1½ tsp baking powder

70 g/2½ oz flaked almonds

1 Preheat the oven to 160°C/325°F/Gas Mark 3. Grease an 18-cm/7-inch square cake tin and line with baking paper.

2 Cut the cherries in half, then put them in a sieve and rinse to remove all the syrup. Pat dry with kitchen paper and set aside.

3 Put the butter, sugar, eggs and ground almonds in a bowl. Sift in the flour and baking powder. Beat thoroughly until smooth, then stir in the cherries. Spoon the mixture into the prepared tin and smooth the top. Sprinkle the flaked almonds over the cake.

4 Bake in the preheated oven for 1½–1¾ hours, until well risen and a skewer inserted into the centre of the cake comes out clean.

5 Leave in the tin for 10 minutes, then turn out onto a wire rack to cool completely.

pear & ginger cake

SERVES 8–10

200 g/7 oz unsalted butter, softened, plus extra for greasing

200 g/7 oz caster sugar

200 g/7 oz self-raising flour, sifted

1 tbsp ground ginger

3 eggs, lightly beaten

450 g/1 lb dessert pears, peeled, cored and thinly sliced

1 tbsp soft light brown sugar

1 Preheat the oven to 180°C/350°F/Gas Mark 4. Grease a 20-cm/8-inch deep round cake tin and line with baking paper.

2 Put 175 g/6 oz of the butter and the caster sugar into a bowl. Sift in the flour and ground ginger and add the eggs. Beat well with a whisk to form a smooth consistency.

3 Spoon the mixture into the prepared tin, smoothing the surface with a palette knife. Arrange the pear slices over the cake mixture. Sprinkle with the brown sugar and dot with the remaining butter.

4 Bake in the preheated oven for 35–40 minutes, or until the cake is golden and feels springy to the touch.

5 Leave the cake to cool slightly in the tin, then turn out onto a wire rack to cool completely.

chocolate lamington cake

SERVES 6

175 g/6 oz butter or margarine, plus extra for greasing

175 g/6 oz caster sugar

3 eggs, lightly beaten

175 g/6 oz self-raising flour

2 tbsp cocoa powder

about 8 tbsp dessicated coconut, to decorate

150 ml/5 fl oz double cream, whipped, to decorate

icing

50 g/1¾ oz plain chocolate, broken into pieces

5 tbsp milk

1 tsp butter

85 g/3 oz icing sugar

1 Preheat the oven to 180°C/350°F/Gas Mark 4. Grease a 450-g/1-lb loaf tin and line with baking paper.

2 Cream the butter and caster sugar together in a bowl until light and fluffy. Gradually add the eggs, beating well after each addition. Sift the flour and cocoa together. Fold into the mixture.

3 Spoon the mixture into the prepared tin and smooth the surface. Bake in the preheated oven for 40 minutes, or until springy to the touch. Leave to cool for 5 minutes in the tin, then turn out onto a wire rack to cool completely.

4 To make the icing, place the chocolate, milk and butter in a heatproof bowl set over a saucepan of gently simmering water. Stir until the chocolate has melted. Add the icing sugar and beat until smooth. Leave the icing to cool until it is thick enough to spread, then spread it all over the cake. Sprinkle with the desiccated coconut and leave to stand until the icing has set.

5 Cut a V-shaped wedge from the top of the cake. Put the cream in a piping bag fitted with a plain or star nozzle. Pipe the cream down the centre of the channel, then replace the wedge of cake. Pipe cream down either side of the wedge of cake.

lemon polenta cake

SERVES 8

200 g/7 oz unsalted butter, plus extra for greasing

200 g/7 oz caster sugar

finely grated rind and juice of 1 large lemon

3 eggs, beaten

140 g/5 oz ground almonds

100 g/3½ oz quick-cook polenta

1 tsp baking powder

crème fraîche, to serve

syrup

juice of 2 lemons

55 g/2 oz caster sugar

2 tbsp water

1 Preheat the oven to 180°C/350°F/Gas Mark 4. Grease a 20-cm/8-inch deep round cake tin and line with baking paper.

2 Beat together the butter and sugar until pale and fluffy. Beat in the lemon rind, lemon juice, eggs and ground almonds. Sift in the polenta and baking powder and stir until evenly mixed. Spoon the mixture into the prepared tin and smooth the surface. Bake in the preheated oven for 30–35 minutes, or until just firm to the touch and golden brown. Remove the cake from the oven and leave to cool in the tin for 20 minutes.

3 To make the syrup, place the lemon juice, sugar and water in a small saucepan. Heat gently, stirring until the sugar has dissolved, then bring to the boil and simmer for 3–4 minutes, or until slightly reduced and syrupy. Turn out the cake onto a wire rack then brush half of the syrup evenly over the surface. Leave to cool completely.

4 Cut the cake into slices, drizzle the extra syrup over the top and serve with crème fraîche.

cranberry & banana loaf

SERVES 8–10

butter, for greasing

175 g/6 oz self-raising flour

½ tsp baking powder

150 g/5½ oz soft light brown sugar

2 bananas, mashed

50 g/1¾ oz mixed peel, chopped

25 g/1 oz mixed nuts, chopped

50 g/1¾ oz dried cranberries

5–6 tbsp orange juice

2 eggs, beaten

150 ml/5 fl oz sunflower oil

75 g/2¾ oz icing sugar, sifted

grated rind of 1 orange, to decorate

1 Preheat the oven to 180°C/350°F/Gas Mark 4. Grease a 900-g/2-lb loaf tin and line with baking paper.

2 Sift the flour and baking powder into a mixing bowl. Stir in the brown sugar, bananas, mixed peel, nuts and cranberries.

3 Mix the orange juice, eggs and oil together in a separate bowl until well combined. Add to the dry ingredients and mix until well blended. Spoon the mixture into the prepared tin.

4 Bake in the preheated oven for about 1 hour, until firm to the touch and a skewer inserted into the centre comes out clean. Turn out onto a wire rack to cool.

5 Mix the icing sugar with a little water and drizzle the icing over the loaf. Sprinkle over the orange rind and leave the icing to set before serving.

banana & lime cake

SERVES 8–10

butter, for greasing

300 g/10½ oz plain flour

1 tsp salt

1½ tsp baking powder

175 g/6 oz soft light brown sugar

1 tsp grated lime rind

1 egg, lightly beaten

1 banana, mashed with 1 tbsp lime juice

150 ml/5 fl oz low-fat natural yogurt

115 g/4 oz sultanas

topping

125 g/4½ oz icing sugar

1–2 tsp lime juice

½ tsp finely grated lime rind

1 Preheat the oven to 180°C/350°F/Gas Mark 4. Grease an 18-cm/7-inch deep round cake tin and line with baking paper.

2 Sift the flour, salt and baking powder into a mixing bowl and stir in the brown sugar and lime rind.

3 Make a well in the centre of the dry ingredients and add the egg, banana, yogurt and sultanas. Mix well until thoroughly incorporated.

4 Spoon the mixture into the prepared tin and smooth the surface. Bake in the preheated oven for 40–45 minutes, until firm to the touch and a skewer inserted into the centre comes out clean. Leave to cool in the tin for 10 minutes, then turn out onto a wire rack.

5 To make the topping, sift the icing sugar into a small bowl and mix with the lime juice to form a soft, but not too runny, icing. Stir in the grated lime rind. Drizzle the lime icing over the cake, letting it run down the sides. Leave to set for 15 minutes.

white chocolate heart cake

SERVES 10

175 g/6 oz plain white flour

1 tbsp baking powder

175 g/6 oz unsalted butter, softened, plus extra for greasing

175 g/6 oz caster sugar

3 eggs, beaten

1 tsp vanilla extract

55 g/2 oz white chocolate, grated

2 tbsp white rum (optional)

crystallized violets, to decorate

frosting

200 g/7 oz white chocolate, broken into pieces

2 tbsp milk

200 ml/7 fl oz double cream

1 Preheat the oven to 160°C/325°F/Gas Mark 3. Grease a 1.5-litre/2¾-pint heart-shaped cake tin.

2 Sift the flour and baking powder into a bowl and add the butter, sugar, eggs and vanilla extract. Beat well until smooth, then stir in the grated chocolate.

3 Spoon the mixture into the prepared tin and smooth the surface with a palette knife. Bake in the preheated oven for 45–55 minutes, or until risen, firm and golden brown. Leave to cool in the tin for 10 minutes, then turn out onto a wire rack to finish cooling.

4 To make the frosting, melt the chocolate with the milk in a heatproof bowl set over a pan of gently simmering water. Remove from the heat and stir until smooth, then leave to cool for 10 minutes. Whip the cream until it holds soft peaks, then fold into the cooled chocolate mixture.

5 Sprinkle the cake with the rum, if using. Spread the frosting over the top and sides of the cake, swirling with a palette knife, then decorate with crystallized violets.

coconut cake

SERVES 6–8

225 g/8 oz self-raising flour

pinch of salt

115 g/4 oz butter, cut into small pieces, plus extra for greasing

115 g/4 oz demerara sugar

100 g/3½ oz grated coconut, plus extra for sprinkling

2 eggs, lightly beaten

4 tbsp milk

1 Preheat the oven to 160°C/325°F/Gas Mark 3. Grease a 900-g/2-lb loaf tin and line with baking paper.

2 Sift the flour and salt into a mixing bowl and rub in the butter with your fingertips until the mixture resembles fine breadcrumbs. Stir in the sugar, coconut, eggs and milk and mix to a soft dropping consistency.

3 Spoon the mixture into the prepared tin and smooth the surface with a palette knife. Bake in the preheated oven for 30 minutes.

4 Remove the cake from the oven and sprinkle with the extra coconut. Return the cake to the oven and bake for an additional 30 minutes, until well risen and golden and a skewer inserted into the centre comes out clean.

5 Leave the cake to cool slightly in the tin, then turn out onto a wire rack to cool completely.

VARIATION

To add lime icing to this cake, sift 175 g/6 oz icing sugar into a bowl and stir in the grated rind and juice of one lime to make a thick icing, adding a few drops of water, if necessary. Spoon the icing over the top of the cake, allowing it to drizzle down the sides of the cake.

2

Sensational Slices & Bars

white chocolate chip brownies

MAKES 8

115 g/4 oz butter, plus extra for greasing

225 g/8 oz white chocolate, roughly chopped

2 eggs

115 g/4 oz soft light brown sugar

115 g/4 oz self-raising flour

75 g/2¾ oz walnut pieces, roughly chopped

1 Preheat the oven to 180°C/350°F/Gas Mark 4. Grease an 18-cm/7-inch square cake tin and line with baking paper.

2 Put the butter and 175 g/6 oz of the chocolate in a heatproof bowl set over a saucepan of gently simmering water. When melted, stir together, then set aside to cool slightly.

3 Whisk the eggs and sugar together, then beat in the cooled chocolate mixture until well mixed. Fold in the flour, the remaining chocolate and the walnuts. Pour the mixture into the prepared tin and smooth the surface.

4 Transfer the tin to the preheated oven and bake for about 30 minutes, until just set. The mixture should still be a little soft in the centre. Leave to cool in the tin, then cut into rectangles before serving.

maple-glazed pistachio brownies

MAKES 16

175 g/6 oz unsalted butter, plus extra for greasing

115 g/4 oz plain chocolate

250 g/9 oz caster sugar

4 eggs, beaten

1 tsp vanilla extract

200 g/7 oz plain flour

85 g/3 oz pistachio nuts, chopped

glaze

115 g/4 oz plain chocolate

115 g/4 oz crème fraîche

2 tbsp maple syrup

1 Preheat the oven to 190°C/375°F/Gas Mark 5. Lightly grease a 30 x 20-cm/12 x 8-inch shallow rectangular baking tin.

2 Place the butter and chocolate in a small pan over a very low heat and stir until melted. Remove from the heat. Whisk the sugar, eggs and vanilla extract together in a large bowl until pale. Beat in the melted chocolate mixture. Fold in the flour evenly, then stir in 55 g/2 oz of the pistachio nuts.

3 Spoon into the prepared tin and smooth the surface. Bake in the preheated oven for 25–30 minutes, or until firm and golden brown.

4 For the glaze, melt the chocolate in a heatproof bowl set over a pan of gently simmering water. Stir in the crème fraîche and maple syrup and beat until smooth and glossy.

5 Spread the glaze evenly over the brownies with a palette knife. Sprinkle with the remaining pistachio nuts and leave until the topping is set.

pecan brownies

MAKES 20

70 g/2½ oz plain chocolate

140 g/5 oz plain flour

¾ tsp bicarbonate of soda

¼ tsp baking powder

225 g/8 oz unsalted butter, plus extra for greasing

100 g/3½ oz demerara sugar, plus extra for sprinkling

½ tsp almond extract

1 egg

55 g/2 oz pecan nuts

1 tsp milk

1 Preheat the oven to 180°C/350°F/Gas Mark 4. Grease a large baking sheet and line with baking paper.

2 Put the chocolate in a heatproof bowl set over a saucepan of gently simmering water and heat until melted. Meanwhile, sift together the flour, bicarbonate of soda and baking powder into a large bowl.

3 In a separate bowl, cream together the butter and sugar, then mix in the almond extract and egg. Remove the chocolate from the heat and stir into the butter mixture. Chop the pecan nuts finely, then add them to the bowl, along with the flour mixture and milk, and stir until well combined.

4 Spoon the mixture onto the prepared baking sheet and smooth the surface. Transfer to the preheated oven and bake for 30 minutes, or until firm to the touch (it should still be a little gooey in the middle). Remove from the oven and leave to cool completely. Remove from the baking sheet and cut into 20 squares. Sprinkle with sugar and serve.

espresso &
walnut brownies

MAKES 9

**115 g/4 oz butter, plus
extra for greasing**

**175 g/6 oz plain chocolate,
roughly chopped**

175 g/6 oz self-raising flour

**2 tbsp instant espresso
coffee powder**

**75 g/2¾ oz walnut pieces,
chopped**

2 eggs, beaten

**150 g/5½ oz light
muscovado sugar**

1 Preheat the oven to 180°C/350°F/Gas Mark 4. Grease and line an 18-cm/7-inch square cake tin with baking paper.

2 Put the butter and 50 g/2 oz of the chocolate in a heatproof bowl. Place the bowl over a pan of simmering water and heat until the butter and chocolate have just melted. Remove from the heat and allow to cool for 10 minutes.

3 Mix together the flour, coffee powder, remaining chocolate and chopped walnuts in a large bowl. Place the eggs and sugar in another bowl and beat with a wooden spoon for a few minutes to break down any lumps of sugar. Add the cooled chocolate mixture, then the flour mixture and beat until thoroughly combined.

4 Transfer the mixture to the prepared tin and place in the centre of the preheated oven. Bake for 30 minutes until the mixture is set, crusted over and cracked but still a little gooey in the centre. Allow to cool in the tin before cutting into nine pieces and serving.

almond slices

MAKES 8

60 g/2¼ oz ground almonds

140 g/5 oz dried milk powder

200 g/7 oz granulated sugar

½ tsp saffron threads

115 g/4 oz unsalted butter, plus extra for greasing

3 eggs, lightly beaten

1 tbsp flaked almonds

1 Preheat the oven to 160°C/325°F/Gas Mark 3. Grease a 20-cm/8-inch shallow square cake tin and line with baking paper.

2 Place the ground almonds, milk powder, sugar and saffron in a large mixing bowl and stir to mix well.

3 Melt the butter in a small saucepan over a low heat. Pour the melted butter over the dry ingredients and mix well with a wooden spoon until thoroughly combined. Add the beaten eggs to the mixture and stir to blend well.

4 Spread the mixture evenly in the prepared tin, sprinkle with the flaked almonds and bake in the preheated oven for 45 minutes, or until a skewer inserted into the centre comes out clean. Remove from the oven, leave to cool slightly and then cut into triangles.

chocolate chip & walnut slices

MAKES 18

115 g/4 oz walnut pieces

**225 g/8 oz butter, plus
extra for greasing**

175 g/6 oz caster sugar

few drops of vanilla extract

225 g/8 oz plain flour

**200 g/7 oz plain chocolate
chips**

1 Preheat the oven to 180°C/350°F/Gas Mark 4. Grease a 20 x 30-cm/8 x 12-inch Swiss roll tin and line with baking paper.

2 Roughly chop the walnut pieces to about the same size as the chocolate chips and set aside.

3 Beat the butter and sugar together until pale and fluffy. Add the vanilla extract, then stir in the flour. Stir in the reserved walnuts and the chocolate chips. Press the mixture into the prepared tin.

4 Bake in the preheated oven for 20–25 minutes, until golden brown. Leave to cool in the tin, then cut into slices.

hazelnut chocolate crunch

MAKES 12

200 g/7 oz rolled oats

55 g/2 oz hazelnuts, lightly toasted and chopped

55 g/2 oz plain flour

115 g/4 oz unsalted butter, plus extra for greasing

85 g/3 oz light muscovado sugar

2 tbsp golden syrup

55 g/2 oz plain chocolate chips

1 Preheat the oven to 180°C/350°F/Gas Mark 4. Grease a 23-cm/9-inch shallow square cake tin.

2 Mix the oats, hazelnuts and flour in a large bowl.

3 Place the butter, sugar and golden syrup in a large saucepan and heat gently until the sugar has dissolved. Pour in the dry ingredients and mix well. Stir in the chocolate chips.

4 Turn the mixture into the prepared tin and bake in the preheated oven for 20–25 minutes, or until golden brown and firm to the touch.

5 Using a knife, mark into 12 triangles and leave to cool in the tin. Cut the triangles with the sharp knife before carefully removing them from the tin.

rocky road bars

MAKES 8

175 g/6 oz milk or plain chocolate

55 g/2 oz butter

100 g/3½ oz shortcake biscuits, broken into pieces

85 g/3 oz mini marshmallows

85 g/3 oz walnuts or peanuts

1 Break the chocolate into squares and place in a heatproof bowl set over a saucepan of gently simmering water and heat until melted. Add the butter and stir until melted and combined. Leave to cool slightly.

2 Stir the broken biscuits, marshmallows and nuts into the chocolate mixture.

3 Line an 18-cm/7-inch square cake tin with baking paper and pour in the chocolate mixture, pressing down with the back of a spoon.

4 Chill in the refrigerator for at least 2 hours, or until firm. Carefully turn out of the tin and cut into eight pieces.

hazelnut squares

MAKES 16

150 g/5½ oz plain flour

pinch of salt

1 tsp baking powder

**75 g/2¾ oz butter, cut into
small pieces, plus extra
for greasing**

**150 g/5½ oz soft light
brown sugar**

1 egg, lightly beaten

4 tbsp milk

**150 g/5½ oz hazelnuts,
halved**

**demerara sugar,
for sprinkling (optional)**

1 Preheat the oven to 180°C/350°F/Gas Mark 4. Grease a
23-cm/9-inch square cake tin and line with baking paper.

2 Sift the flour, salt and baking powder into a large bowl.
Rub in the butter with your fingertips until the mixture
resembles fine breadcrumbs. Stir in the brown sugar. Add
the egg, milk and hazelnuts to the mixture and stir well until
thoroughly combined.

3 Spoon the mixture into the prepared cake tin, spreading
it out evenly, and smooth the surface. Sprinkle with
demerara sugar, if using.

4 Bake in the preheated oven for about 25 minutes, or until
the mixture is firm to the touch.

5 Leave to cool for 10 minutes in the tin, then loosen
the edges with a round-bladed knife and turn out onto
a wire rack. Cut into squares and leave to cool completely
before serving.

macadamia nut caramel squares

MAKES 16

280 g/10 oz plain flour

175 g/6 oz soft light brown sugar

115 g/4 oz butter, plus extra for greasing

115 g/4 oz macadamia nuts, roughly chopped

topping

115 g/4 oz butter

100 g/3½ oz soft light brown sugar

200 g/7 oz milk chocolate chips

1 Preheat the oven to 180°C/350°F/Gas Mark 4. Grease a 30 x 20-cm/12 x 8-inch rectangular baking tin.

2 To make the base, sift the flour into a bowl and stir in the sugar. Rub in the butter with your fingertips until the mixture resembles fine breadcrumbs.

3 Press the mixture into the base of the prepared tin. Sprinkle over the macadamia nuts.

4 To make the topping, put the butter and sugar in a saucepan and slowly bring the mixture to the boil, stirring constantly. Boil for 1 minute, stirring constantly, then carefully pour the mixture over the macadamia nuts.

5 Bake in the preheated oven for about 20 minutes, until the caramel topping is bubbling. Remove from the oven and immediately sprinkle the chocolate chips evenly on top. Leave for 2–3 minutes, until the chocolate chips start to melt, then, using the blade of a knife, swirl the chocolate over the top. Leave to cool in the tin, then cut into squares.

chocolate coconut squares

MAKES 9

225 g/8 oz plain chocolate digestive biscuits

75 g/2¾ oz butter or margarine, plus extra for greasing

200 ml/7 fl oz canned evaporated milk

1 egg, beaten

1 tsp vanilla extract

2 tbsp caster sugar

40 g/1½ oz self-raising flour, sifted

125 g/4½ oz grated coconut

50 g/1¾ oz plain chocolate, melted

1 Preheat the oven to 190°C/375°F/Gas Mark 5. Grease a 20-cm/8-inch shallow square cake tin and line with baking paper.

2 Place the biscuits in a polythene bag and crush with a rolling pin or process them in a food processor. Melt the butter in a saucepan and stir in the crushed biscuits thoroughly. Press the mixture into the base of the prepared tin.

3 Beat together the evaporated milk, egg, vanilla extract and sugar until smooth. Stir in the flour and grated coconut. Pour over the biscuit layer and use a palette knife to smooth the surface. Bake in the preheated oven for 30 minutes, or until the coconut topping has become firm and just golden.

4 Leave to cool in the cake tin for about 5 minutes, then cut into squares. Leave to cool completely in the tin. Carefully remove the squares from the tin and place them on a cutting board. Drizzle the melted chocolate over the squares and leave to set before serving.

blueberry granola bars

MAKES 12

115 g/4 oz dried blueberries

225 g/8 oz rolled oats

40 g/1½ oz soft light brown sugar

50 g/1¾ oz pecan nuts, chopped

25g/1 oz sunflower seeds

1 tbsp sesame seeds

¼ tsp ground cinnamon

115 g/4 oz golden syrup

115 g/4 oz butter, plus extra for greasing

1 Preheat the oven to 180°C/350°F/Gas Mark 4. Grease an 18 x 28-cm/7 x 11-inch baking tin.

2 Put the blueberries, oats, sugar, pecan nuts, seeds and cinnamon into a large bowl.

3 Heat the golden syrup and butter in a pan over a low heat until just melted. Stir in the dry ingredients to coat thoroughly. Transfer the mixture to the prepared tin and smooth the surface.

4 Place in the preheated oven and bake for 20 minutes until golden. Remove from the oven and leave to cool for 5 minutes before marking into 12 bars.

5 Allow to cool completely in the tin and then cut through the markings to create 12 bars.

apricot flapjacks

MAKES 10

175 g/6 oz margarine, plus extra for greasing

85 g/3 oz demerara sugar

55 g/2 oz clear honey

140 g/5 oz dried apricots, chopped

2 tsp sesame seeds

225 g/8 oz rolled oats

1 Preheat the oven to 180°C/350°F/Gas Mark 4. Grease a 26 x 17-cm/10½ x 6½-inch shallow rectangular baking tin.

2 Put the margarine, sugar and honey into a small saucepan over a low heat and heat until the ingredients have melted together – do not boil. When the ingredients are well combined, stir in the apricots, sesame seeds and oats.

3 Spoon the mixture into the prepared tin and smooth the surface with the back of a spoon. Bake in the preheated oven for 20–25 minutes, or until golden brown.

4 Remove from the oven, cut into bars and leave to cool completely before removing from the tin.

fruity flapjacks

MAKES 14

140 g/5 oz rolled oats

115 g/4 oz demerara sugar

85 g/3 oz raisins

**115 g/4 oz butter, melted,
plus extra for greasing**

1 Preheat the oven to 190°C/375°F/Gas Mark 5. Grease a 28 x 18-cm/11 x 7-inch shallow rectangular baking tin.

2 Combine the oats, sugar and raisins with the butter, stirring well. Spoon the mixture into the prepared tin and press down firmly with the back of a spoon. Bake in the preheated oven for 15–20 minutes, or until golden.

3 Using a sharp knife, mark into 14 bars, then leave to cool in the tin for 10 minutes. Carefully transfer the bars to a wire rack to cool completely.

apricot blondies

MAKES 12

350 g/12 oz white chocolate

85 g/3 oz unsalted butter, plus extra for greasing

1 tsp vanilla extract

3 eggs, beaten

140 g/5 oz light muscovado sugar

115 g/4 oz self-raising flour

85 g/3 oz macadamia nuts, roughly chopped

100 g/3½ oz dried apricots, roughly chopped

1 Preheat the oven to 190°C/375°F/Gas Mark 5. Grease a 28 x 18-cm/11 x 7-inch rectangular baking tin and line with baking paper.

2 Chop half the chocolate into small chunks. Melt the remaining chocolate with the butter in a small pan over a very low heat and stir until melted. Remove from the heat and stir in the vanilla extract.

3 Whisk the eggs and sugar together in a large bowl until pale. Beat in the melted chocolate mixture. Fold in the flour evenly, then stir in the macadamia nuts, apricots and chopped chocolate.

4 Spoon into the prepared tin and smooth the surface. Bake in the preheated oven for 25–30 minutes, or until firm and golden brown.

5 Leave to cool in the tin. Turn out when completely cool and cut into triangles.

fudge blondies

MAKES 9

**125 g/4½ oz butter,
softened, plus extra for
greasing**

**200 g/7 oz soft light brown
sugar**

2 large eggs, lightly beaten

1 tsp vanilla extract

250 g/9 oz plain flour

1 tsp baking powder

**125 g/4½ oz soft butter
fudge, chopped into
small pieces**

**75 g/2¾ oz macadamia
nuts, roughly chopped**

icing sugar, for dusting

1 Preheat the oven to 180°C/350°F/Gas Mark 4. Grease a shallow 20-cm/8-inch square baking tin and line with baking paper.

2 Place the butter and brown sugar in a large bowl and whisk together until pale and creamy. Gradually whisk in the eggs and vanilla extract. Sift the flour and baking powder into the mixture and beat together until well mixed. Add the fudge pieces and chopped nuts and stir together until combined. Spoon the mixture into the prepared tin and smooth the surface.

3 Bake in the preheated oven for 40–45 minutes, or until risen and golden brown. Leave to cool in the tin, then dust with sifted icing sugar to decorate and cut into squares.

butterscotch blondies

MAKES 9

115 g/4 oz plain flour

½ tsp baking powder

⅛ tsp bicarbonate of soda

¼ tsp salt

**115 g/4 oz butter, melted,
plus extra for greasing**

175 g/6 oz brown sugar

4 tbsp granulated sugar

**1 egg plus 1 egg yolk,
beaten together**

1 tsp vanilla extract

**85 g/3 oz butterscotch
chips**

**40 g/1½ oz milk chocolate
chips**

**25 g/1 oz dry-roasted
cashew nuts, chopped**

1 Preheat the oven to 180°C/350°F/Gas Mark 4. Grease a 20 x 20-cm/8 x 8-inch baking tin or ovenproof dish.

2 Sift together the flour, baking powder, bicarbonate of soda and salt into a large bowl.

3 Whisk together the melted butter and the sugars in another bowl until combined, then whisk in the beaten eggs and vanilla extract. Stir in the dry ingredients with a wooden spoon, then fold in the butterscotch chips, chocolate chips and chopped cashew nuts.

4 Using a spatula, scrape the mixture into the prepared tin or dish and smooth to spread out evenly. Bake in the preheated oven for 35 minutes, until the top is golden brown and a skewer inserted into the centre comes out clean. Leave to cool completely before cutting into nine squares.

upside-down toffee apple squares

115 g/4 oz unsalted butter, plus extra for greasing

115 g/6 oz light muscovado sugar

2 eggs, beaten

200 g/7 oz plain flour

1 tsp baking powder

½ tsp bicarbonate of soda

1½ tsp ground mixed spice

2 eating apples, peeled and coarsely grated

85 g/3 oz hazelnuts, chopped

toffee apple topping

85 g/3 oz light muscovado sugar

55 g/2 oz unsalted butter

1 dessert apple, cored and thinly sliced

1 Preheat the oven to 180°C/350°F/Gas Mark 4. Grease a 23-cm/9-inch shallow square cake tin.

2 For the topping, place the sugar and butter in a small pan and heat gently, stirring, until melted. Pour into the prepared tin. Arrange the dessert apple slices over the mixture.

3 Place the butter and sugar in a bowl and beat well until pale and fluffy. Beat in the eggs gradually.

4 Sift together the flour, baking powder, bicarbonate of soda and mixed spice, and fold into the mixture. Stir in the grated eating apples and hazelnuts.

5 Pour into the prepared tin and bake in the preheated oven for 35–40 minutes, until firm and golden. Cool in the tin for 10 minutes, then turn out and cut into squares.

strawberry & chocolate slices

MAKES 16

225 g/8 oz plain flour

1 tsp baking powder

100 g/3½ oz caster sugar

85 g/3 oz soft light brown sugar

225 g/8 oz unsalted butter, plus extra for greasing

150 g/5½ oz rolled oats

225 g/8 oz strawberry jam

100 g/3½ oz plain chocolate chips

25 g/1 oz flaked almonds

1 Preheat the oven to 190°C/375°F/Gas Mark 5. Grease a 30 x 20-cm/12 x 8-inch deep rectangular baking tin and line with baking paper.

2 Sift the flour and baking powder into a large bowl. Add the caster sugar and brown sugar and mix well. Add the butter and rub in with your fingertips until the mixture resembles breadcrumbs. Stir in the oats.

3 Press three quarters of the mixture into the base of the prepared tin. Bake in the preheated oven for 10 minutes.

4 Spread the jam over the cooked base, then sprinkle over the chocolate chips. Mix the remaining mixture with the almonds. Sprinkle evenly over the chocolate chips and press down gently.

5 Return to the oven and bake for a further 20–25 minutes, until golden brown. Leave to cool in the tin, then cut into slices.

date, pistachio & honey slices

MAKES 12

250 g/9 oz dates, stoned and chopped

2 tbsp lemon juice

2 tbsp water

85 g/3 oz pistachio nuts, chopped

2 tbsp clear honey

milk to glaze

pastry

225 g/8 oz plain flour, plus extra for dusting

25 g/1 oz golden caster sugar

150 g/5½ oz butter

4–5 tbsp cold water to mix

1 Place the dates, lemon juice and water in a saucepan and bring to the boil, stirring. Remove from the heat. Stir in the pistachio nuts and 1 tbsp honey. Cover and leave to cool.

2 Preheat the oven to 200°C/400°F/Gas Mark 6. For the pastry, place the flour, sugar and butter in a food processor and process to fine crumbs. Mix in just enough cold water to bind to a soft, not sticky, dough.

3 Roll out the pastry on a floured surface to two 30 x 20-cm/12 x 8-inch rectangles. Place one on a baking sheet. Spread the date and nut mixture to within 1 cm/½ inch of the edge. Top with the remaining pastry.

4 Press to seal, trim the edges and mark into 12 slices. Glaze with milk. Bake in the preheated oven for 20–25 minutes, until golden. Brush with the remaining honey and turn out onto a wire rack to cool.

5 Cut into slices and serve.

gingerbread squares

MAKES 24

**90 g/3¼ oz butter or
margarine, plus extra
for greasing**

**55 g/2 oz dark muscovado
sugar**

5 tbsp black treacle

1 egg white

1 tsp almond extract

**175 g/6 oz plain flour, plus
extra for dusting**

¼ tsp bicarbonate of soda

¼ tsp baking powder

pinch of salt

½ tsp mixed spice

½ tsp ground ginger

**125 g/4½ oz dessert apples,
cooked and
finely chopped**

1 Preheat the oven to 180°C/350°F/Gas Mark 4. Grease a large baking sheet and line with baking paper.

2 Put the butter, sugar, treacle, egg white and almond extract into a food processor and process until smooth.

3 In a separate bowl, sift the flour, bicarbonate of soda, baking powder, salt, mixed spice and ginger together. Add to the creamed mixture and beat together thoroughly. Stir in the chopped apples. Pour the mixture onto the prepared baking sheet.

4 Transfer to the preheated oven and bake for 10 minutes, or until golden brown. Remove from the oven and cut into 24 pieces. Transfer to a wire rack to cool completely before serving.

ginger-topped fingers

MAKES 16

225 g/8 oz plain flour

1 tsp ground ginger

85 g/3 oz golden caster sugar

175 g/6 oz butter, plus extra for greasing

topping

1 tbsp golden syrup

55 g/2 oz butter

4 tbsp icing sugar

1 tsp ground ginger

1 Preheat the oven to 180°C/350°F/Gas Mark 4. Grease a 28 x 18-cm/11 x 7-inch rectangular baking tin.

2 Sift the flour and ginger into a bowl and stir in the caster sugar. Rub in the butter with your fingertips until the mixture begins to stick together.

3 Press the mixture into the prepared tin and smooth the surface with a palette knife. Bake in the preheated oven for 40 minutes, or until very lightly browned.

4 To make the topping, place the golden syrup and butter in a small saucepan over a low heat and stir until melted. Stir in 2 tablespoons of the icing sugar and all of the ginger. Remove the shortbread base from the oven and pour the topping over it while both are still hot.

5 Place the remaining icing sugar in a small bowl and stir in just enough water to form a thin icing. Spoon into a small piping bag fitted with a small plain nozzle and pipe horizontal lines over the ginger topping. Use a cocktail stick to pull vertical lines through the icing to create a feathered effect. Leave to cool slightly in the tin, then cut into slices. Transfer to a wire rack to cool completely.

malted chocolate slices

MAKES 16

MAKES 16

85 g/3 oz butter, plus extra for greasing

2 tbsp golden syrup

2 tbsp malted chocolate drink

225 g/8 oz malted milk biscuits

75 g/2¾ oz milk or plain chocolate, broken into pieces

2 tbsp icing sugar

2 tbsp milk

1 Grease a shallow 18-cm/7-inch round cake tin or flan tin and line with baking paper.

2 Place the butter, golden syrup and malted chocolate drink in a small saucepan and heat gently, stirring all the time until the butter has melted and the mixture is well combined.

3 Crush the biscuits in a polythene bag with a rolling pin, or process them in a food processor. Stir the biscuit crumbs into the chocolate mixture and mix well. Press the mixture into the prepared tin and then chill in the refrigerator until firm.

4 Place the chocolate pieces in a small heatproof bowl with the sugar and the milk. Place the bowl over a saucepan of gently simmering water and stir until the chocolate melts and the mixture is combined.

5 Spread the chocolate icing over the biscuit base and let the icing set in the tin. Using a sharp knife, cut into triangles to serve.

carrot streusel bars

MAKES 15

115 g/4 oz unsalted butter, softened, plus extra for greasing

350 g/12 oz light muscovado sugar

2 eggs, beaten

1 tsp vanilla extract

175 g/6 oz plain flour

½ tsp bicarbonate of soda

½ tsp baking powder

85 g/3 oz sultanas

125 g/4½ oz carrots, finely grated

55 g/2 oz chopped walnuts

streusel topping

40 g/1½ oz finely chopped walnuts

40 g/1½ oz dark muscovado sugar

15 g/½ oz plain flour

½ tsp ground cinnamon

15 g/½ oz unsalted butter, melted

1 Preheat the oven to 180°C/350°F/Gas Mark 4. Grease a 30 x 20-cm/12 x 8-inch shallow rectangular baking tin and line with baking paper.

2 Cream together the butter and light sugar until pale. Beat in the eggs and vanilla extract. Sift the flour, bicarbonate of soda and baking powder into the mixture and fold in evenly. Stir in the sultanas, carrots and walnuts.

3 Spoon the mixture into the prepared tin. Mix together all the topping ingredients to make a crumbly mixture and sprinkle evenly over the cake mixture.

4 Bake in the preheated oven for 45–55 minutes, or until golden brown and just firm to the touch. Cool in the tin, then cut into bars.

VARIATION

To create hazelnut streusel bars instead, replace the sultanas and walnuts with raisins and chopped toasted hazelnuts, and the cinnamon with ground nutmeg.

3

Splendid Small Cakes & Cookies

chocolate chip cupcakes

MAKES 18

85 g/3 oz butter, softened

100 g/3½ oz caster sugar

2 eggs, lightly beaten

2 tbsp milk

55 g/2 oz plain chocolate chips

225 g/8 oz self-raising flour

25 g/1 oz cocoa powder, plus extra for dusting

icing

225 g/8 oz white chocolate, broken into pieces

150 g/5½ oz cream cheese

1 Preheat the oven to 200°C/400°F/Gas Mark 6. Place 18 paper cases in a bun tin.

2 Beat together the butter and sugar until pale and fluffy. Gradually add the eggs, beating well after each addition. Add a little of the flour if the mixture starts to curdle. Add the milk, then fold in the chocolate chips.

3 Sift together the flour and cocoa and fold into the mixture with a metal spoon or palette knife. Divide the batter equally between the paper cases and smooth the surfaces.

4 Bake in the preheated oven for 20 minutes, or until well risen and springy to the touch. Transfer to a wire rack to cool.

5 To make the icing, melt the chocolate in a heatproof bowl set over a saucepan of gently simmering water. Cool slightly. Beat the cream cheese until softened, then beat in the melted chocolate. Spread the icing over each cake and leave to chill for 1 hour. Dust with a little cocoa before serving.

devil's food chocolate cupcakes

MAKES 18

50 g/1¾ oz soft margarine

115 g/4 oz soft dark brown sugar

2 large eggs

115 g/4 oz plain flour

½ tsp bicarbonate of soda

25 g/1 oz cocoa powder

125 ml/4 fl oz soured cream

chocolate caraque, to decorate

icing

125 g/4½ oz plain chocolate, broken into pieces

2 tbsp caster sugar

150 ml/5 fl oz soured cream

1 Preheat the oven to 180°C/350°F/Gas Mark 4. Place 18 paper cases in a bun tin.

2 Put the margarine, brown sugar, eggs, flour, bicarbonate of soda and cocoa powder in a large bowl and, using an electric hand-held whisk, beat together until just smooth. Using a metal spoon, fold in the soured cream. Spoon the mixture into the paper cases.

3 Bake the cupcakes in the preheated oven for 20 minutes, or until well risen and firm to the touch. Transfer to a wire rack to cool.

4 To make the icing, put the chocolate into a heatproof bowl set over a saucepan of gently simmering water and heat until melted, stirring occasionally. Remove from the heat and allow to cool slightly, then whisk in the caster sugar and soured cream until combined. Spread the icing over the tops of the cupcakes and leave to set in the refrigerator before serving. Serve decorated with chocolate caraque.

lemon butterfly cupcakes

MAKES 12

115 g/4 oz self-raising flour

½ tsp baking powder

115 g/4 oz butter, softened

115 g/4 oz caster sugar

2 eggs, beaten

**finely grated rind of
¾ lemon**

2–4 tbsp milk

icing sugar, for dusting

filling

55 g/2 oz butter

115 g/4 oz icing sugar

1 tbsp lemon juice

1 Preheat the oven to 190°C/375°F/Gas Mark 5. Place 12 paper cases in a bun tin.

2 Sift the flour and baking powder into a bowl. Add the butter, caster sugar, eggs, lemon rind and enough milk to give a medium-soft consistency. Beat the mixture thoroughly until smooth, then divide between the paper cases.

3 Bake in the preheated oven for 15–20 minutes, or until well risen and golden. Transfer to a wire rack to cool.

4 To make the filling, place the butter in a bowl. Sift in the icing sugar and add the lemon juice. Beat well until smooth and creamy.

5 When the cakes are completely cooled, use a sharp-pointed vegetable knife to cut a circle from the top of each cake, then cut each circle in half. Spoon a little buttercream filling on top of each cake and press the two semi-circular pieces into it to resemble wings. Dust the cakes with icing sugar before serving.

cranberry cupcakes

MAKES 12

75 g/2¾ oz butter, softened, or soft margarine

100 g/3½ oz caster sugar

1 large egg, lightly beaten

2 tbsp milk

100 g/3½ oz self-raising flour

1 tsp baking powder

75 g/2¾ oz frozen cranberries

1 Preheat the oven to 180°C/350°F/Gas Mark 4. Place 12 paper cases in a bun tin.

2 Place the butter and sugar in a large bowl and beat together until light and fluffy, then gradually beat in the egg and stir in the milk. Sift in the flour and baking powder and fold into the mixture. Gently fold in the frozen cranberries. Spoon the mixture into the paper cases.

3 Bake in the preheated oven for 15–20 minutes, or until well risen and golden brown. Transfer to a wire rack to cool completely.

blueberry muffins

MAKES 12

280 g/10 oz plain flour

1 tbsp baking powder

⅛ tsp salt

115 g/4 oz soft light brown sugar

150 g/5½ oz frozen blueberries

2 eggs

250 ml/9 fl oz milk

6 tbsp sunflower oil or 85 g/3 oz butter, melted and cooled

1 tsp vanilla extract

finely grated rind of 1 lemon

1 Preheat the oven to 200°C/400°F/Gas Mark 6. Place 12 paper cases in a muffin tin.

2 Sift together the flour, baking powder and salt into a large bowl. Stir in the sugar and blueberries.

3 Lightly beat the eggs in a large jug or bowl then beat in the milk, oil, vanilla extract and lemon rind. Make a well in the centre of the dry ingredients and pour in the beaten liquid ingredients. Stir gently until just combined; do not over-mix.

4 Spoon the mixture into the paper cases. Bake in the preheated oven for about 20 minutes, until well risen, golden brown and firm to the touch.

5 Leave the muffins in the tin for 5 minutes, then serve warm or transfer to a wire rack to cool.

chocolate chunk muffins

MAKES 12

280 g/10 oz plain flour

1 tbsp baking powder

⅛ tsp salt

115 g/4 oz caster sugar

175 g/6 oz chocolate chunks

2 eggs

250 ml/9 fl oz milk

6 tbsp sunflower oil or 85 g/3 oz butter, melted and cooled

1 tsp vanilla extract

1 Preheat the oven to 200°C/400°F/Gas Mark 6. Place 12 paper cases in a muffin tin.

2 Sift together the flour, baking powder and salt into a large bowl. Stir in the sugar and chocolate chunks.

3 Lightly beat the eggs in a large jug or bowl then beat in the milk, oil and vanilla extract.

4 Make a well in the centre of the dry ingredients and pour in the beaten liquid ingredients. Stir gently until just combined; do not over-mix.

5 Spoon the mixture into the paper cases. Bake in the preheated oven for about 20 minutes, until well risen, golden brown and firm to the touch. Leave the muffins in the tin for 5 minutes, then serve warm or transfer to a wire rack to cool.

jam muffins

MAKES 12

**oil or melted butter,
for greasing**

280 g/10 oz plain flour

1 tbsp baking powder

⅛ tsp salt

115 g/4 oz caster sugar

2 eggs

200 ml/7 fl oz milk

**6 tbsp sunflower oil or
85 g/3 oz butter,
melted and cooled**

1 tsp vanilla extract

**4 tbsp strawberry jam or
raspberry jam**

topping

115 g/4 oz butter

**150 g/5½ oz granulated
sugar**

1 Preheat the oven to 200°C/400°F/Gas Mark 6. Grease a 12-cup muffin tin.

2 Sift together the flour, baking powder and salt into a large bowl. Stir in the caster sugar.

3 Lightly beat the eggs in a large jug or bowl then beat in the milk, oil and vanilla extract. Make a well in the centre of the dry ingredients and pour in the beaten liquid ingredients. Stir gently until just combined; do not over-mix.

4 Spoon half of the mixture into the prepared muffin tin. Add a teaspoon of jam to the centre of each, then spoon in the remaining mixture. Bake in the preheated oven for about 20 minutes, until well risen, golden brown and firm to the touch.

5 Meanwhile, prepare the topping. Melt the butter. Spread the granulated sugar in a wide, shallow bowl. When the muffins are baked, leave in the tin for 5 minutes. Dip the tops of the muffins in the melted butter then roll in the sugar. Serve warm or transfer to a wire rack to cool.

muesli muffins

MAKES 12

140 g/5 oz plain flour

1 tbsp baking powder

280 g/10 oz unsweetened muesli

115 g/4 oz soft light brown sugar

2 eggs

250 ml/9 fl oz buttermilk

6 tbsp sunflower oil

1 Preheat the oven to 200°C/400°F/Gas Mark 6. Place 12 paper cases in a muffin tin.

2 Sift together the flour and baking powder into a large bowl. Stir in the muesli and sugar.

3 Place the eggs in a large jug or bowl and beat lightly, then beat in the buttermilk and oil. Make a well in the centre of the dry ingredients and pour in the beaten liquid ingredients. Stir gently until just combined; do not over-mix. Spoon the mixture into the paper cases.

4 Bake in the preheated oven for about 20 minutes, or until well risen, golden brown and firm to the touch. Leave to cool in the tin for 5 minutes, then serve warm or transfer to a wire rack to cool.

cherry & sultana scones

MAKES 8

225 g/8 oz self-raising flour, plus extra for dusting

1 tbsp caster sugar

pinch of salt

85 g/3 oz butter, cut into small pieces, plus extra for greasing

3 tbsp glacé cherries, chopped

3 tbsp sultanas

1 egg, lightly beaten

3 tbsp milk

1 Preheat the oven to 220°C/425°F/Gas Mark 7. Grease a baking sheet and line with baking paper.

2 Sift the flour, sugar and salt into a mixing bowl and rub in the butter with your fingertips until the mixture resembles breadcrumbs.

3 Stir in the glacé cherries and sultanas. Add the egg. Reserve 1 tablespoon of the milk for glazing, then add the remainder to the mixture. Mix well together to form a soft dough.

4 On a lightly floured work surface, roll out the dough to a thickness of 2 cm/¾ inch and cut out eight circles using a 5-cm/2-inch round cutter.

5 Place the scones on the prepared baking sheet and brush the tops with the reserved milk. Bake in the preheated oven for 8–10 minutes, or until the scones are golden brown. Transfer the scones to a wire rack to cool completely.

almond & raspberry jam drops

MAKES 25

225 g/8 oz butter, softened, plus extra for greasing

140 g/5 oz caster sugar

1 egg yolk, lightly beaten

2 tsp almond extract

280 g/10 oz plain flour

pinch of salt

55 g/2 oz almonds, toasted and chopped

55 g/2 oz chopped mixed peel

4 tbsp raspberry jam

1 Preheat the oven to 190°C/375°F/Gas Mark 5. Grease two baking sheets and line with baking paper.

2 Put the butter and sugar into a bowl and mix well with a wooden spoon, then beat in the egg yolk and almond extract. Sift together the flour and salt into the mixture, add the almonds and mixed peel and stir until thoroughly combined.

3 Scoop up tablespoons of the mixture and shape into balls with your hands, then put them onto the prepared baking sheets, spaced well apart. Use the dampened handle of a wooden spoon to make a hollow in the centre of each ball and fill the hollows with raspberry jam.

4 Bake in the preheated oven for 12–15 minutes, until golden brown. Leave to cool on the baking sheets for 5–10 minutes, then, using a palette knife, carefully transfer to wire racks to cool completely.

chocolate viennese fingers

MAKES 18

115 g/4 oz unsalted butter, plus extra for greasing

6 tbsp icing sugar

225 g/8 oz self-raising flour, sifted

3 tbsp cornflour

200 g/7 oz plain chocolate, broken into pieces

1 Preheat the oven to 190°C/375°F/Gas Mark 5. Grease two baking sheets and line with baking paper.

2 Beat the butter and sugar in a mixing bowl until light and fluffy. Gradually beat in the flour and cornflour. Put 75 g/2¾ oz of the chocolate in a heatproof bowl set over a saucepan of gently simmering water and stir until melted. Beat the melted chocolate into the mixture.

3 Place in a piping bag fitted with a large star nozzle and pipe fingers about 5 cm/2 inches long onto the prepared baking sheets, allowing room for the biscuits to spread during cooking.

4 Bake in the preheated oven for 12–15 minutes. Leave to cool slightly on the baking sheets, then transfer to a wire rack and leave to cool completely.

5 Melt the remaining chocolate as above. Dip one end of each biscuit in the chocolate, allowing the excess to drip back into the bowl. Place the biscuits on a sheet of baking paper and leave the chocolate to set before serving.

marshmallow s'mores

MAKES ABOUT 15

225 g/8 oz butter, softened

140 g/5 oz caster sugar

2 tsp finely grated orange rind

1 egg yolk, lightly beaten

250 g/9 oz plain flour

25 g/1 oz cocoa powder

½ tsp ground cinnamon

pinch of salt

30 yellow marshmallows, halved horizontally

300 g/10½ oz plain chocolate, broken into pieces

4 tbsp orange marmalade

15 walnut halves, to decorate

1 Place the butter, sugar and orange rind in a large bowl and beat together until light and fluffy, then beat in the egg yolk. Sift together the flour, cocoa, cinnamon and salt into the mixture and stir until combined. Halve the dough, shape into balls, wrap in clingfilm and chill for 30–60 minutes.

2 Preheat the oven to 190°C/375°F/Gas Mark 5. Line two large baking sheets with baking paper. Unwrap the dough and roll out between two sheets of baking paper. Cut out cookies with a 6-cm/2½-inch fluted round cutter and place them on the prepared baking sheets, spaced well apart. Bake in the preheated oven for 10–15 minutes. Leave to cool for 5 minutes. Turn half the cookies upside down and put four marshmallow halves on each. Bake these cookies with marshmallows on for a further 1–2 minutes. Leave all the cookies on wire racks for 30 minutes.

3 Place the chocolate in a heatproof bowl, set the bowl over a saucepan of gently simmering water and heat until melted. Line a baking sheet with baking paper. Spread the marmalade over the undersides of the uncovered cookies and place them on top of the marshmallow-covered cookies. Dip the cookies in the melted chocolate to coat. Place a walnut half in the centre of each cookie and leave to set.

meringues

MAKES 12

4 egg whites

pinch of salt

**125 g/4½ oz granulated
sugar**

125 g/4½ oz caster sugar

**300 ml/10 fl oz double
cream, lightly whipped,
to serve**

1 Preheat the oven to 120°C/250°F/Gas Mark ½. Line three baking sheets with baking paper.

2 Place the egg whites and salt in a large clean bowl and, using an electric hand-held whisk or balloon whisk, whisk until stiff. (You should be able to turn the bowl upside down without any movement from the whisked egg whites.) Whisk in the granulated sugar, a little at a time; the meringue should begin to look glossy at this stage.

3 Sprinkle in the caster sugar, a little at a time, and continue whisking until all the sugar has been incorporated and the meringue is thick, white and forms peaks.

4 Transfer the meringue mixture to a piping bag fitted with a 2-cm/¾-inch star nozzle. Carefully pipe about 24 small whirls of the mixture onto the prepared baking sheets.

5 Bake in the preheated oven for 1½ hours, or until the meringues are pale golden in colour and can be easily lifted off the paper. Leave them to cool overnight in the switched-off oven. Just before serving, sandwich the meringues together in pairs with the cream and arrange on a serving plate.

lemon jumbles

MAKES 50

75 g/2¾ oz butter, softened,
plus extra for greasing

115 g/4 oz caster sugar

grated rind of 1 lemon

1 egg, lightly beaten

4 tbsp lemon juice

350 g/12 oz plain flour,
plus extra for dusting

1 tsp baking powder

1 tbsp milk

icing sugar, for dusting

1 Preheat the oven to 160°C/325°F/Gas Mark 3. Grease several baking sheets and line with baking paper.

2 In a mixing bowl, cream together the butter, caster sugar and lemon rind, until pale and fluffy. Add the egg and lemon juice, a little at a time, beating well after each addition.

3 Sift the flour and baking powder into the creamed mixture and blend together. Add the milk, mixing to form a firm dough.

4 Turn the dough out onto a lightly floured work surface and divide into about 50 equal-sized pieces. Roll each piece into a sausage shape with your hands and twist in the middle to make an 'S' shape or curls.

5 Place the biscuits on the prepared baking sheets and bake in the preheated oven for 15–20 minutes. Transfer to wire racks and leave to cool completely. Dust generously with icing sugar before serving.

chocolate chip shortbread

MAKES 8

115 g/4 oz plain flour

55 g/2 oz cornflour

55 g/2 oz golden caster sugar

115 g/4 oz butter, diced, plus extra for greasing

40 g/1½ oz plain chocolate chips

1 Preheat the oven to 160°C/325°F/Gas Mark 3. Grease a 23-cm/9-inch loose-based fluted tart tin.

2 Sift the flour and cornflour into a large bowl. Stir in the sugar, then add the butter and rub it in with your fingertips until the mixture starts to bind together.

3 Turn into the prepared tart tin and press evenly over the base. Prick the surface with a fork. Sprinkle with the chocolate chips and press lightly into the surface.

4 Bake in the preheated oven for 35–40 minutes, or until cooked but not brown. Mark into eight portions with a sharp knife. Leave to cool in the tin for 10 minutes, then transfer to a wire rack to cool completely.

chocolate caramel shortbread

MAKES 12

115 g/4 oz butter, plus extra for greasing

175 g/6 oz plain flour

55 g/2 oz golden caster sugar

filling and topping

175 g/6 oz butter

115 g/4 oz golden caster sugar

3 tbsp golden syrup

400 g/14 oz canned condensed milk

200 g/7 oz plain chocolate, broken into pieces

1 Preheat the oven to 180°C/350°F/Gas Mark 4. Grease and line a 23-cm/9-inch shallow square cake tin with baking paper.

2 Place the butter, flour and sugar in a food processor and process until it begins to bind together. Press the mixture into the prepared tin and smooth the top. Bake in the preheated oven for 20–25 minutes, or until golden.

3 Meanwhile, make the filling. Place the butter, sugar, golden syrup and condensed milk in a saucepan and heat gently until the sugar has dissolved. Bring to the boil and simmer for 6–8 minutes, stirring constantly, until the mixture becomes very thick. Pour over the shortbread base and leave to chill in the refrigerator until firm.

4 To make the topping, place the chocolate in a heatproof bowl, set the bowl over a saucepan of gently simmering water and heat until melted, then spread over the caramel. Chill in the refrigerator until set. Cut the shortbread into 12 pieces with a sharp knife and serve.

oaty raisin & hazelnut cookies

MAKES 30

55 g/2 oz raisins, chopped

125 ml/4 fl oz orange juice

225 g/8 oz butter, softened, plus extra for greasing

140 g/5 oz caster sugar

1 egg yolk, lightly beaten

2 tsp vanilla extract

225 g/8 oz plain flour

pinch of salt

55 g/2 oz rolled oats

55 g/2 oz hazelnuts, chopped

whole hazelnuts, to decorate

1 Preheat the oven to 190°C/375°F/Gas Mark 5. Grease two baking sheets and line with baking paper.

2 Put the raisins in a bowl, add the orange juice and leave to soak for 10 minutes. Put the butter and sugar into a bowl and mix well with a wooden spoon, then beat in the egg yolk and vanilla extract.

3 Sift together the flour and salt into the mixture and add the oats and chopped hazelnuts. Drain the raisins, add them to the mixture and stir until thoroughly combined.

4 Scoop up tablespoons of the mixture and place them in mounds on the prepared baking sheets, spaced well apart. Flatten slightly and place a whole hazelnut in the centre of each cookie.

5 Bake in the preheated oven for 12–15 minutes, until golden brown. Leave to cool on the baking sheets for 5–10 minutes, then, using a palette knife, carefully transfer the cookies to wire racks to cool completely.

white chocolate cookies

MAKES 24

115 g/4 oz butter, softened, plus extra for greasing

115 g/4 oz soft light brown sugar

1 egg, beaten

250 g/9 oz self-raising flour

pinch of salt

125 g/4½ oz white chocolate, chopped

50 g/1¾ oz Brazil nuts, chopped

1 Preheat the oven to 190°C/375°F/Gas Mark 5. Grease several baking sheets.

2 In a large mixing bowl, cream together the butter and sugar until light and fluffy.

3 Gradually add the egg to the creamed mixture, beating well after each addition.

4 Sift the flour and salt into the creamed mixture and blend well. Stir in the chocolate and Brazil nuts.

5 Place heaped teaspoonfuls of the mixture on the prepared baking sheets, spaced well apart. Bake in the preheated oven for 10–12 minutes, or until just golden brown.

6 Transfer the cookies to wire racks to cool completely.

chewy golden cookies

MAKES 30

175 g/6 oz butter or margarine, plus extra for greasing

250 g/9 oz soft light brown sugar

350 g/12 oz golden syrup

3 egg whites

250 g/9 oz rolled oats

280 g/10 oz plain flour

pinch of salt

1 tsp baking powder

2 tbsp icing sugar, to decorate

1 Preheat the oven to 180°C/350°F/Gas Mark 4. Grease several large baking sheets and line with baking paper.

2 In a large mixing bowl, blend the butter, sugar, golden syrup and egg whites together. Gradually add the oats, flour, salt and baking powder and mix thoroughly.

3 Drop 30 rounded tablespoonfuls of the mixture onto the prepared baking sheets, spaced well apart, and transfer to the preheated oven. Bake for 12 minutes, or until the biscuits are light brown.

4 Transfer to wire racks to cool. Mix the icing sugar with a few drops of water to form a thin icing, drizzle over the biscuits and leave to set.

black & white cookies

MAKES 20

115 g/4 oz unsalted butter, plus extra for greasing

1 tsp vanilla extract

175 g/6 oz caster sugar

2 eggs, beaten

300 g/10½ oz plain flour

½ tsp baking powder

200 ml/7 fl oz milk

icing

225 g/8 oz icing sugar

125 ml/4 fl oz double cream

⅛ tsp vanilla extract

75 g/2¾ oz plain chocolate, broken into pieces

1 Preheat the oven to 190°C/375°F/Gas Mark 5. Grease three baking sheets. Place the butter, vanilla extract and caster sugar in a large bowl. Beat the mixture with a whisk until light and fluffy and then beat in the eggs one at a time.

2 Sift the flour and baking powder and fold into the creamed mixture, loosening with milk as you go until both are used up and the mixture is of dropping consistency.

3 Drop heaped tablespoonfuls of the mixture, spaced well apart, on the prepared baking sheets. Place in the preheated oven and bake for 15 minutes until turning golden at the edges and light to the touch. Transfer to wire racks to cool completely.

4 To make the icing, put the icing sugar in a bowl and mix in half the cream and the vanilla extract. The consistency should be thick but spreadable. Using a palette knife, spread half of each cookie with white icing. Now, melt the chocolate in a bowl over a pan of simmering water. Remove from the heat and stir in the remaining cream. Spread the dark icing over the uncoated cookie halves.

chocolate sprinkle cookies

MAKES 30

225 g/8 oz butter, softened, plus extra for greasing

140 g/5 oz caster sugar

1 egg yolk, lightly beaten

2 tsp vanilla extract

225 g/8 oz plain flour, plus extra for dusting

55 g/2 oz cocoa powder

pinch of salt

topping

200 g/7 oz white chocolate, broken into pieces

85 g/3 oz chocolate vermicelli, to decorate

1 Put the butter and sugar into a bowl and mix well with a wooden spoon, then beat in the egg yolk and vanilla extract. Sift together the flour, cocoa powder and salt into the mixture and stir until thoroughly combined. Halve the dough, roll each piece into a ball, wrap in clingfilm and chill in the refrigerator for 30–60 minutes.

2 Preheat the oven to 190°C/375°F/Gas Mark 5. Grease two baking sheets and line with baking paper.

3 Unwrap the dough and roll out between two pieces of baking paper to about 5 mm/¼ inch thick and stamp out 30 cookies with a 6–7-cm/2½–2¾-inch fluted round cutter. Put them on the prepared baking sheets, spaced well apart.

4 Bake in the preheated oven for 10–12 minutes. Leave to cool on the baking sheets for 5–10 minutes, then, using a palette knife, carefully transfer the cookies to wire racks to cool completely.

5 Put the white chocolate into a heatproof bowl set over a pan of gently simmering water until melted, then immediately remove from the heat. Spread the melted chocolate over the cookies, leave to cool slightly, then sprinkle with the chocolate vermicelli. Leave to cool and set.

mocha walnut cookies

MAKES 16

115 g/4 oz butter, softened, plus extra for greasing

115 g/4 oz light muscovado sugar

85 g/3 oz caster sugar

1 tsp vanilla extract

1 tbsp instant coffee granules, dissolved in 1 tbsp hot water

1 egg

175 g/6 oz plain flour

½ tsp baking powder

¼ tsp bicarbonate of soda

55 g/2 oz milk chocolate chips

55 g/2 oz walnuts, roughly chopped

1 Preheat the oven to 180°C/350°F/Gas Mark 4. Grease two baking sheets and line with baking paper.

2 Put the butter, muscovado sugar and caster sugar in a bowl and beat until light and fluffy. Put the vanilla extract, coffee and egg in a separate bowl and whisk together.

3 Gradually add the coffee mixture to the butter and sugar mixture, beating until fluffy. Sift the flour, baking powder and bicarbonate of soda into the mixture and fold in carefully. Fold in the chocolate chips and walnuts.

4 Spoon heaped teaspoonfuls of the mixture onto the prepared baking sheets, spaced well apart. Bake in the preheated oven for 10–15 minutes, until crisp on the outside but still soft inside. Leave to cool on the baking sheets for 2 minutes, then transfer to wire racks to cool completely.

sticky ginger cookies

MAKES 20

225 g/8 oz butter, softened, plus extra for greasing

140 g/5 oz golden caster sugar

1 egg yolk, lightly beaten

55 g/2 oz roughly chopped stem ginger, plus 1 tbsp syrup from the jar

280 g/10 oz plain flour

pinch of salt

55 g/2 oz plain chocolate chips

1 Put the butter and sugar into a bowl and mix well with a wooden spoon, then beat in the egg yolk and ginger syrup.

2 Sift together the flour and salt into the mixture, add the stem ginger and chocolate chips and stir until thoroughly combined. Shape the mixture into a log, wrap in clingfilm and chill in the refrigerator for 30–60 minutes.

3 Preheat the oven to 190°C/375°F/Gas Mark 5. Grease two baking sheets and line with baking paper.

4 Unwrap the log and cut it into 5-mm/¼-inch slices with a sharp serrated knife. Put them onto the prepared baking sheets, spaced well apart.

5 Bake in the preheated oven for 12–15 minutes, until golden brown. Leave to cool on the baking sheets for 5–10 minutes, then, using a palette knife, carefully transfer the cookies to wire racks to cool completely.

rum & raisin sandwich cookies

MAKES 15

100 g/3½ oz raisins

150 ml/5 fl oz rum

225 g/8 oz butter, softened, plus extra for greasing

140 g/5 oz caster sugar

1 egg yolk, lightly beaten

280 g/10 oz plain flour

pinch of salt

orange filling

175 g/6 oz icing sugar

85 g/3 oz butter, softened

2 tsp finely grated orange rind

1 tsp rum

few drops of yellow food colouring (optional)

1 Put the raisins into a bowl. Pour in the rum and leave to soak for 15 minutes, then drain, reserving any remaining rum. Preheat the oven to 190°C/375°F/Gas Mark 5. Grease two baking sheets and line with baking paper.

2 Put the butter and caster sugar into a bowl and mix well with a wooden spoon, then beat in the egg yolk and 2 teaspoons of the reserved rum. Sift together the flour and salt into the mixture, add the raisins and stir until thoroughly combined.

3 Scoop up tablespoons of the dough and put them on the prepared baking sheets, spaced well apart. Flatten gently and smooth the tops with the tines of a fork.

4 Bake in the preheated oven for 10–15 minutes, until light golden brown. Leave to cool on the baking sheets for 5–10 minutes, then, using a palette knife, carefully transfer to wire racks to cool completely.

5 To make the orange filling, sift the icing sugar into a bowl, add the butter, orange rind, rum and food colouring, if using, and beat well until smooth. Spread the filling over half the cookies and top with the remaining cookies.

VARIATION

To create a chocolate filling instead, heat 125 ml/4 fl oz double cream to boiling point and pour over 125 g/4½ oz chopped plain chocolate, then mix together until smooth. Cool and chill until thick, then use to sandwich the biscuits together.

4

Delicious Desserts

mississippi mud pie

140 g/5 oz digestive biscuits

85 g/3 oz pecan nuts, finely chopped

1 tbsp soft light brown sugar

½ tsp ground cinnamon

85 g/3 oz butter, melted

filling

225 g/8 oz butter or margarine, plus extra for greasing

175 g/6 oz plain chocolate, chopped

125 ml/4 fl oz golden syrup

4 large eggs, beaten

85 g/3 oz pecan nuts, finely chopped

1 Preheat the oven to 180°C/350°F/Gas Mark 4. Lightly grease a 23-cm/9-inch loose-based round cake tin.

2 To make the crumb crust, put the digestive biscuits, pecan nuts, sugar and cinnamon into a food processor and process until fine crumbs form – do not overprocess to a powder. Add the melted butter and process again until moistened.

3 Tip the crumb mixture into the prepared cake tin and press over the base and about 4 cm/1½ inches up the side of the tin. Cover the tin and chill while making the filling.

4 To make the filling, put the butter, chocolate and golden syrup into a saucepan over a low heat and stir until melted and blended. Leave to cool, then beat in the eggs and pecan nuts.

5 Pour the filling into the chilled crumb crust and smooth the surface. Bake in the preheated oven for 30 minutes, or until just set but still soft in the centre. Transfer to a wire rack to cool. Serve at room temperature or chilled.

blueberry cheesecake

SERVES 8–10

sunflower oil, for brushing

85 g/3 oz butter

200 g/7 oz digestive biscuits, crushed

400 g/14 oz cream cheese

2 large eggs

140 g/5 oz caster sugar

1½ tsp vanilla extract

450 ml/16 fl oz soured cream

blueberry topping

55 g/2 oz caster sugar

4 tbsp water

250 g/9 oz fresh blueberries

1 tsp arrowroot

1 Preheat the oven to 190°C/375°F/Gas Mark 5. Brush a 20-cm/8-inch round springform cake tin with oil.

2 Melt the butter in a saucepan over a low heat. Stir in the biscuits, then spread over the base of the tin.

3 Place the cream cheese, eggs, 100 g/3½ oz of the sugar and ½ teaspoon of the vanilla extract in a food processor. Process until smooth. Pour over the biscuit base and smooth the top. Place on a baking sheet and bake in the preheated oven for 20 minutes, until set. Remove from the oven and leave for 20 minutes. Leave the oven switched on.

4 Mix the soured cream with the remaining sugar and vanilla extract in a bowl. Spoon over the cheesecake. Return it to the oven for 10 minutes, leave to cool, then cover with clingfilm and chill in the refrigerator for 8 hours, or overnight.

5 To make the topping, place the sugar in a saucepan with 2 tablespoons of the water over a low heat and stir until the sugar has dissolved. Increase the heat, add the blueberries, cover and cook for a few minutes, or until they begin to soften. Remove from the heat. Mix the arrowroot and remaining water in a bowl, add to the blueberries and stir until smooth. Return to a low heat. Cook until the juice thickens and turns translucent. Leave to cool. Remove the cheesecake from the tin 1 hour before serving. Spoon over the blueberry topping and chill until ready to serve.

ricotta cheesecake

SERVES 6–8

pastry

175 g/6 oz plain flour, plus extra for dusting

3 tbsp caster sugar

pinch of salt

115 g/4 oz unsalted butter, chilled and diced

1 egg yolk

filling

450 g/1 lb ricotta cheese

125 ml/4 fl oz double cream

2 eggs, plus 1 egg yolk

85 g/3 oz caster sugar

finely grated rind of 1 lemon

finely grated rind of 1 orange

1 To make the pastry, sift the flour with the sugar and salt onto a work surface and make a well in the centre. Add the diced butter and egg yolk to the well and, using your fingertips, gradually work into the flour mixture until fully incorporated. Gather up the dough and knead very lightly. Cut off about one quarter, wrap in clingfilm and chill in the refrigerator. Press the remaining dough into the base of a 23-cm/9-inch loose-based tart tin. Chill for 30 minutes. Meanwhile, preheat the oven to 190°C/375°F/Gas Mark 5.

2 To make the filling, beat the ricotta cheese with the cream, eggs and extra egg yolk, sugar, lemon rind and orange rind. Cover with clingfilm and place in the refrigerator until required. Prick the base of the pastry case all over with a fork. Line with baking paper, fill with baking beans and bake in the preheated oven for 15 minutes.

3 Remove the pastry case from the oven and take out the baking paper and beans. Stand the tin on a wire rack and set aside to cool. Spoon the ricotta mixture into the pastry case and smooth the surface. Roll out the reserved pastry on a lightly floured surface and cut it into strips. Arrange the strips over the filling in a lattice pattern, brushing the overlapping ends with water so that they stick.

4 Bake for a further 30–35 minutes, until the top of the cheesecake is golden and the filling has set. Cool on a wire rack before removing from the tin.

baked lemon cheesecake

SERVES 6–8

**55 g/2 oz butter,
plus extra for greasing**

**175 g/6 oz gingernut
biscuits, crushed**

3 lemons

300 g/10½ oz ricotta cheese

**200 g/7 oz Greek-style
yogurt**

4 eggs

1 tbsp cornflour

100 g/3½ oz caster sugar

**strips of lemon zest,
to decorate**

icing sugar, for dusting

1 Preheat the oven to 180°C/350°F/Gas Mark 4. Grease a 20-cm/8-inch round springform cake tin and line with baking paper.

2 Melt the butter and stir in the biscuit crumbs. Press into the base of the prepared cake tin. Chill until firm.

3 Meanwhile, finely grate the rind and squeeze the juice from the lemons. Add the ricotta, yogurt, eggs, cornflour and caster sugar, and whisk until a smooth batter is formed.

4 Carefully spoon the mixture into the tin. Bake in the preheated oven for 40–45 minutes, or until just firm and golden brown.

5 Cool the cheesecake completely in the tin, then run a knife around the edge to loosen and turn out onto a serving plate. Decorate with lemon zest and dust with icing sugar.

sticky toffee pudding

SERVES 4

75 g/2¾ oz sultanas

**150 g/5½ oz dates, stoned
and chopped**

1 tsp bicarbonate of soda

**25 g/1 oz butter, plus extra
for greasing**

**200 g/7 oz soft dark
brown sugar**

2 eggs

**200 g/7 oz self-raising
flour, sifted**

sticky toffee sauce

25 g/1 oz butter

**175 ml/6 fl oz double
cream**

**200 g/7 oz soft dark
brown sugar**

1 Put the sultanas, dates and bicarbonate of soda into a heatproof bowl. Cover with boiling water and leave to soak.

2 Preheat the oven to 180°C/350°F/Gas Mark 4. Grease a 18-cm/7-inch square cake tin. Put the butter in a separate bowl, add the sugar and mix well. Beat in the eggs then fold in the flour. Drain the soaked fruits, add to the bowl and mix.

3 Spoon the mixture evenly into the prepared cake tin. Transfer to the preheated oven and bake for 35–40 minutes, or until a skewer inserted into the centre comes out clean.

4 About 5 minutes before the end of the cooking time, make the sauce. Melt the butter in a saucepan over a medium heat. Stir in the cream and sugar and bring to the boil, stirring constantly. Lower the heat and simmer for 5 minutes.

5 Cut the cake into squares and turn out onto serving plates. Pour over the sauce and serve.

strawberry shortcake

SERVES 8

175 g/6 oz self-raising flour

100 g/3½ oz unsalted butter, diced and chilled, plus extra for greasing

75 g/2¾ oz caster sugar

1 egg yolk

1 tbsp rosewater

600 ml/1 pint whipping cream, lightly whipped

225 g/8 oz strawberries, hulled and quartered, plus a few whole strawberries to decorate

icing sugar, for dusting

1 Preheat the oven to 190°C/375°F/Gas Mark 5. Grease two baking sheets and line with baking paper.

2 To make the shortcakes, sift the flour into a bowl. Rub in the butter with your fingers until the mixture resembles breadcrumbs. Stir in the caster sugar, then add the egg yolk and rosewater and mix to form a soft dough.

3 Divide the dough in half. Roll out each piece into a 19-cm/7½-inch round and transfer each one to a prepared baking sheet. Crimp the edges of the dough and prick all over with a fork.

4 Bake in the preheated oven for 15 minutes, until lightly golden. Transfer the shortcakes to a wire rack to cool.

5 Mix the cream with the strawberry quarters and spoon on top of one of the shortcakes. Cut the remaining shortcake round into wedges, then place on top of the cream. Dust with icing sugar and decorate with whole strawberries.

rhubarb crumble

SERVES 6

900 g/2 lb rhubarb

115 g/4 oz caster sugar

**grated rind and
juice of 1 orange**

crumble topping

225 g/8 oz plain flour

115 g/4 oz unsalted butter

**115 g/4 oz soft light
brown sugar**

1 tsp ground ginger

1 Preheat the oven to 190°C/375°F/Gas Mark 5.

2 Cut the rhubarb into 2.5-cm/1-inch lengths and place in a 1.7-litre/3-pint ovenproof dish with the caster sugar, orange rind and orange juice.

3 To make the crumble topping, place the flour in a mixing bowl and rub in the butter with your fingertips until the mixture resembles breadcrumbs. Stir in the brown sugar and ginger.

4 Spread the crumble topping evenly over the fruit and press down lightly using a fork. Place on a baking sheet and bake in the centre of the preheated oven for 25–30 minutes, until the topping is golden brown. Serve warm.

pecan pie

pastry

200 g/7 oz plain flour, plus extra for dusting

115 g/4 oz unsalted butter

2 tbsp caster sugar

a little cold water

filling

70 g/2½ oz unsalted butter

100 g/3½ oz light muscovado sugar

140 g/5 oz golden syrup

2 large eggs, beaten

1 tsp vanilla extract

115 g/4 oz pecan nuts

1 For the pastry, place the flour in a bowl and rub in the butter with your fingertips until it resembles fine breadcrumbs. Stir in the caster sugar and add enough cold water to mix to a firm dough. Wrap in clingfilm and chill for 15 minutes, until firm enough to roll out.

2 Preheat the oven to 200°C/400°F/Gas Mark 6. Roll out the pastry on a lightly floured surface and use to line a 23-cm/9-inch loose-based round tart tin. Prick the base with a fork. Chill for 15 minutes.

3 Place the tart tin on a baking sheet and line with baking paper and baking beans. Bake blind in the preheated oven for 10 minutes. Remove the baking beans and paper and bake for a further 5 minutes. Reduce the oven temperature to 180°C/350°F/Gas Mark 4.

4 For the filling, place the butter, muscovado sugar and golden syrup in a saucepan and heat gently until melted. Remove from the heat and quickly beat in the eggs and vanilla extract. Roughly chop the pecan nuts and stir into the mixture. Pour into the pastry case and bake for 35–40 minutes, until the filling is just set.

traditional apple pie

SERVES 6

pastry

350 g/12 oz plain flour

pinch of salt

85 g/3 oz butter or margarine, cut into small pieces

85 g/3 oz lard or white vegetable fat, cut into small pieces

beaten egg or milk, for glazing

filling

750 g–1 kg/1 lb 10 oz– 2 lb 4 oz cooking apples, peeled, cored and sliced

125 g/4½ oz caster sugar, plus extra for sprinkling

½–1 tsp ground cinnamon, mixed spice or ground ginger

1 To make the pastry, sift the flour and salt into a mixing bowl. Add the butter and lard and rub in with your fingertips until the mixture resembles fine breadcrumbs. Add about 6 tablespoons of water and gather the mixture together into a dough. Wrap the dough and chill in the refrigerator for 30 minutes.

2 Preheat the oven to 220°C/425°F/Gas Mark 7. Roll out almost two thirds of the pastry thinly and use to line a deep 23-cm/9-inch pie dish.

3 Mix the apples with the sugar and spice and pack into the pastry case; the filling can come up above the rim. Add 1–2 tablespoons of water if needed, particularly if the apples are not very juicy.

4 Roll out the remaining pastry to form a lid. Dampen the edges of the pie rim with water and position the lid, pressing the edges firmly together. Trim and crimp the edges. Use the trimmings to cut out leaves or other shapes to decorate the top of the pie. Dampen and attach. Glaze the top of the pie with beaten egg, make 1–2 slits in the top and place the pie on a baking sheet.

5 Bake in the preheated oven for 20 minutes, then reduce the temperature to 180°C/350°F/Gas Mark 4 and bake for a further 30 minutes, or until the pastry is a light golden brown. Serve hot or cold, sprinkled with sugar.

spiced apple tart

SERVES 6–8

pastry

200 g/7 oz plain flour, plus extra for dusting

100 g/3½ oz butter, diced, plus extra for greasing

50 g/1¾ oz icing sugar, sifted

finely grated rind of 1 lemon

1 egg yolk, beaten

3 tbsp milk

filling

3 cooking apples

2 tbsp lemon juice

finely grated rind of 1 lemon

150 ml/5 fl oz honey

175 g/6 oz fresh white or wholemeal breadcrumbs

1 tsp mixed spice

pinch of ground nutmeg

1 To make the pastry, sift the flour into a bowl. Rub in the butter, then mix in the sugar, lemon rind, egg yolk and milk. Knead briefly, then wrap in clingfilm and chill in the refrigerator for 30 minutes.

2 Preheat the oven to 200°C/400°F/Gas Mark 6. Grease a 20-cm/8-inch tart tin. Roll out the pastry to a thickness of 5 mm/¼ inch and use to line the tin.

3 To make the filling, core two of the apples and grate them into a bowl. Add 1 tablespoon of the lemon juice and all the lemon rind, along with the honey, breadcrumbs and mixed spice. Mix together well. Spoon evenly into the pastry case.

4 Core and slice the remaining apple, and use to decorate the top of the tart. Brush the apple slices with the remaining lemon juice, then sprinkle over the nutmeg.

5 Bake in the preheated oven for 35 minutes, or until firm. Serve warm.

forest fruits pie

SERVES 6

pastry

200 g/7 oz plain flour, plus extra for dusting

25 g/1 oz ground hazelnuts

100 g/3½ oz butter, cut into small pieces, plus extra for greasing

finely grated rind of 1 lemon

1 egg yolk, beaten

4 tbsp milk

filling

250 g/9 oz blueberries

250 g/9 oz raspberries

250 g/9 oz blackberries

100 g/3½ oz caster sugar

1 To make the filling, put the berries in a saucepan with 3 tablespoons of the sugar and simmer, stirring frequently, for 5 minutes. Remove the pan from the heat.

2 Sift the flour into a bowl, then add the hazelnuts. Rub in the butter with your fingertips until the mixture resembles breadcrumbs, then stir in the remaining sugar from the filling ingredients. Add the lemon rind, egg yolk and 3 tablespoons of the milk and mix. Turn out onto a lightly floured work surface and knead briefly. Wrap and chill in the refrigerator for 30 minutes.

3 Preheat the oven to 190°C/375°F/Gas Mark 5. Grease a 20-cm/8-inch pie dish. Roll out two thirds of the pastry to a thickness of 5 mm/¼ inch and use it to line the dish.

4 Spoon the berry mixture into the pastry case. Brush the rim with water, then roll out the remaining pastry and use it to cover the pie. Trim and crimp round the edge, then make two small slits in the top and decorate with leaf shapes cut out from the dough trimmings. Brush all over with the remaining milk. Bake in the preheated oven for 40 minutes. Serve hot.

amaretti & peaches

SERVES 6

1 egg white

85 g/3 oz caster sugar

85 g/3 oz ground almonds

⅛ tsp almond extract

3 peaches or nectarines, sliced

2 tbsp almond liqueur

300 g/10½ oz vanilla ice cream (6 scoops), to serve

1 Preheat the oven to 170°C/325°F/Gas Mark 3. Line a baking sheet with baking paper.

2 Place the egg white in a large bowl and whisk until stiff. Gently fold the sugar, ground almonds and almond extract gently into the egg white with a large metal spoon until you have a smooth paste.

3 Roll teaspoonfuls of the mixture lightly between the palms of your hands to form 12 walnut-sized balls. Place the balls 2 cm/¾ inch apart on the prepared baking sheet. Bake in the preheated oven for approximately 20 minutes until cracked and light golden. Leave to cool, but keep the oven on.

4 Meanwhile, place the sliced peaches and 1 tablespoon of almond liqueur in a heatproof dish. Cover and bake in the preheated oven for 20 minutes until just tender. Remove from the oven, sprinkle with the remaining almond liqueur and leave to cool. Drain the peaches, reserving the juices, and arrange the peach slices in a fan on six side plates. Sandwich a scoop of ice cream between two amaretti and place on top of each peach fan. Spoon over the reserved peach juices and serve immediately.

blueberry clafoutis

**25 g/1 oz butter, plus extra
for greasing**

125 g/4½ oz caster sugar

3 eggs

60 g/2¼ oz plain flour

250 ml/9 fl oz single cream

½ tsp ground cinnamon

450 g/1 lb blueberries

icing sugar, for dusting

single cream, to serve

1 Preheat the oven to 180°C/350°F/Gas Mark 4. Grease a
1-litre/1¾-pint ovenproof dish.

2 Put the butter in a bowl with the caster sugar and whisk
together until fluffy. Add the eggs and beat together
well. Mix in the flour, then gradually stir in the cream
followed by the cinnamon. Continue to stir until smooth.

3 Arrange the blueberries in the base of the prepared dish,
then pour the flour mixture over the top. Transfer to
the preheated oven and bake for about 30 minutes, or until
puffed and golden.

4 Dust lightly with icing sugar and serve warm with cream.

chestnut, maple syrup & pecan tart

SERVES 6

pastry

125 g/4½ oz plain flour, plus extra for dusting

pinch of salt

75 g/2¾ oz cold butter, cut into pieces, plus extra for greasing

filling

1 kg/2 lb 4 oz canned sweetened chestnut purée

300 ml/10 fl oz double cream

25 g/1 oz butter

2 tbsp maple syrup

150 g/5½ oz pecan nuts

1 Grease a 23-cm/9-inch loose-based fluted tart tin. Sift the flour and salt into a food processor, add the butter and process until the mixture resembles fine breadcrumbs. Tip the mixture into a large bowl and add a little cold water, just enough to bring the dough together.

2 Turn out onto a lightly floured work surface and roll out the pastry 8 cm/3¼ inches larger than the tin. Carefully lift the pastry into the tin and press to fit. Roll the rolling pin over the tin to neaten the edges and trim the excess pastry. Fit a piece of baking paper into the tart case, fill with baking beans and chill in the refrigerator for 30 minutes. Meanwhile, preheat the oven to 190°C/375°F/Gas Mark 5.

3 Remove the tart tin from the refrigerator and bake in the preheated oven for 15 minutes, then remove the beans and paper and bake for a further 10 minutes.

4 Empty the chestnut purée into a large bowl. Whip the cream until stiff and fold into the chestnut purée. Spoon into the cold pastry case and chill for 2 hours.

5 Melt the butter with the maple syrup and when bubbling add the pecan nuts and stir for 1–2 minutes. Spoon onto baking paper and cool. When ready to serve, arrange the pecan nuts on the chestnut cream.

tarte au citron

pastry

175 g/6 oz plain flour, plus extra for dusting

½ tsp salt

115 g/4 oz cold unsalted butter, diced

1 egg yolk, beaten with 2 tbsp ice-cold water

filling

grated rind of 2–3 large lemons

150 ml/5 fl oz lemon juice

100 g/3½ oz caster sugar

125 ml/4 fl oz double cream or crème fraîche

3 large eggs

3 large egg yolks

icing sugar, for dusting

fresh raspberries, to serve

1 To make the pastry, sift the flour and salt into a large bowl. Add the butter and rub it in with your fingertips until the mixture resembles fine breadcrumbs. Add the egg yolk and water and stir to mix to a dough. Gather the dough into a ball, wrap in clingfilm and leave to chill for at least 1 hour.

2 Preheat the oven to 200°C/400°F/Gas Mark 6. Roll the dough out on a lightly floured work surface and use to line a 23–25-cm/9–10-inch loose-based tart tin. Prick the base of the pastry all over with a fork and line with baking paper and baking beans.

3 Bake in the preheated oven for 15 minutes, until the pastry looks set. Remove the paper and beans. Reduce the oven temperature to 190°C/375°F/Gas Mark 5.

4 To make the filling, beat the lemon rind, lemon juice and caster sugar together until blended. Slowly beat in the cream, then beat in the eggs and yolks, one by one.

5 Place the pastry case on a baking sheet and pour in the filling. Transfer to the preheated oven and bake for 20 minutes, until the filling is set. Leave to cool completely on a wire rack. Dust with icing sugar and serve with raspberries.

banoffee pie

SERVES 6–8

filling

3 x 400 g/14 oz canned sweetened condensed milk

4 ripe bananas

juice of ½ lemon

1 tsp vanilla extract

75 g/2¾ oz plain chocolate, grated

475 ml/17 fl oz double cream, whipped

biscuit crust

85 g/3 oz butter, melted, plus extra for greasing

150 g/5½ oz digestive biscuits, crushed

25 g/1 oz almonds, toasted and ground

25 g/1 oz hazelnuts, toasted and ground

1 Place the unopened cans of milk in a large saucepan and add enough water to cover them. Bring to the boil, then reduce the heat and simmer for 2 hours, topping up the water level to keep the cans covered. Carefully lift out the hot cans from the pan and leave to cool.

2 Preheat the oven to 180°C/350°F/Gas Mark 4. To make the crust, place the butter in a bowl and add the crushed digestive biscuits and ground nuts. Mix together well, then press the mixture evenly into the base and sides of a greased 23-cm/9-inch tart tin. Bake in the preheated oven for 10–12 minutes. Leave to cool.

3 Peel and slice the bananas and place in a bowl. Squeeze over the juice from the lemon, add the vanilla extract and mix together. Spread the banana mixture over the biscuit crust in the tin, then spoon over the contents of the cooled cans of condensed milk.

4 Sprinkle over 50 g/1¾ oz of the chocolate, then top with a layer of whipped cream. Sprinkle over the remaining grated chocolate and serve the pie at room temperature.

chocolate brownie roulade

SERVES 6

butter, for greasing

150 g/5½ oz plain chocolate, broken into pieces

3 tbsp water

175 g/6 oz caster sugar

5 eggs, separated

25 g/1 oz raisins, chopped

25 g/1 oz pecan nuts, chopped

pinch of salt

icing sugar, for dusting

300 ml/10 fl oz double cream, lightly whipped

1 Preheat the oven to 180°C/350°F/Gas Mark 4. Grease a 30 x 20-cm/12 x 8-inch Swiss roll tin and line with baking paper.

2 Melt the chocolate with the water in a small saucepan over a low heat until the chocolate has melted. Leave to cool.

3 In a bowl, whisk the caster sugar and egg yolks for 2–3 minutes with an electric hand-held whisk until thick and pale. Fold in the cooled chocolate, raisins and pecan nuts. In a separate bowl, whisk the egg whites with the salt. Fold one quarter of the egg whites into the chocolate mixture, then fold in the rest of the whites, working lightly and quickly.

4 Transfer the mixture to the prepared tin and bake in the preheated oven for 25 minutes, until risen and just firm to the touch. Leave to cool before covering with a sheet of baking paper and a damp clean tea towel. Leave until cold.

5 Turn the roulade out onto another piece of baking paper dusted with icing sugar and carefully remove the lining paper. Spread the cream over the roulade. Starting from a short end, roll the sponge away from you using the paper to guide you. Trim the ends of the roulade to make a neat finish and transfer to a serving plate. Leave to chill in the refrigerator. Dust with icing sugar before serving.

chocolate truffle torte

SERVES 10

butter, for greasing

50 g/1¾ oz caster sugar

2 eggs

40 g/1½ oz plain flour

25 g/1 oz cocoa powder

4 tbsp strong black coffee

2 tbsp brandy

cocoa powder and icing sugar, for dusting

truffle topping

600 ml/1 pint whipping cream

425 g/15 oz plain chocolate, broken into pieces

1 Preheat the oven to 220°C/425°F/Gas Mark 7. Grease a 23-cm/9-inch round cake tin and line with baking paper.

2 Put the caster sugar and eggs in a heatproof bowl set over a saucepan of gently simmering water. Whisk together until pale and resembling the texture of mousse. Sift in the flour and cocoa and fold gently into the mixture. Pour into the prepared tin and bake in the preheated oven for 7–10 minutes, or until risen and firm to the touch.

3 Transfer to a wire rack to cool. Wash and dry the tin and replace the cooled cake in the tin. Mix together the coffee and brandy and brush over the cake.

4 To make the truffle topping, put the cream in a bowl and whisk until just holding very soft peaks. Put the chocolate in a heatproof bowl set over a saucepan of gently simmering water until melted. Carefully fold the cooled melted chocolate into the cream. Pour the chocolate mixture over the sponge. Chill until set.

5 To decorate the torte, sift cocoa over the top and remove carefully from the tin. Using strips of baking paper, sift bands of icing sugar over the torte to create a striped pattern. Cut into slices with a hot knife.

raspberry & chocolate cake

SERVES 10

**225 g/8 oz butter,
plus extra for greasing**

250 g/9 oz plain chocolate

1 tbsp strong black coffee

5 eggs

**90 g/3¼ oz golden
caster sugar**

**90 g/3¼ oz plain
flour, sifted**

1 tsp ground cinnamon

**150 g/5½ oz fresh
raspberries,
plus extra to serve**

cocoa powder, for dusting

whipped cream, to serve

1 Preheat the oven to 160°C/325°F/Gas Mark 3. Grease a 23-cm/9-inch round cake tin and line with baking paper.

2 Put the butter, chocolate and coffee in a heatproof bowl set over a saucepan of gently simmering water and heat until melted. Stir and leave to cool slightly.

3 Put the eggs and sugar in a bowl and beat until thick and pale. Gently fold in the chocolate mixture. Sift the flour and cinnamon into a bowl, then fold into the chocolate mixture. Pour into the prepared tin and sprinkle the raspberries evenly over the top.

4 Bake in the preheated oven for 35–45 minutes, until the cake is well risen and springy to the touch. Leave to cool in the tin for 15 minutes before turning out onto a large plate. Dust with cocoa and serve with raspberries and whipped cream.

key lime pie

biscuit crust

175 g/6 oz digestive or ginger biscuits

2 tbsp caster sugar

½ tsp ground cinnamon

70 g/2½ oz butter, melted, plus extra for greasing

filling

400 g/14 oz canned condensed milk

125 ml/4 fl oz freshly squeezed lime juice

finely grated rind of 3 limes

4 egg yolks

whipped cream, to serve

1 Preheat the oven to 160°C/325°F/Gas Mark 3. Grease a 23-cm/9-inch round tart tin, about 4 cm/1½ inches deep.

2 To make the biscuit crust, put the biscuits, sugar and cinnamon in a food processor and process until fine crumbs form – do not overprocess to a powder. Add the melted butter and process again until moistened.

3 Tip the crumb mixture into the prepared tart tin and press evenly into the base and sides. Place the tart tin on a baking sheet and bake in the preheated oven for 5 minutes. Meanwhile, beat the condensed milk, lime juice, lime rind and egg yolks together in a bowl until well blended.

4 Remove the tart tin from the oven, pour the filling into the biscuit crust and spread out to the edges. Return to the oven for a further 15 minutes, or until the filling is set around the edges but still wobbly in the centre. Leave to cool completely on a wire rack, then cover and chill for at least 2 hours. Serve spread thickly with whipped cream.

peach melba meringue roulade

SERVES 8

sunflower oil, for brushing

coulis

**350 g/12 oz fresh
raspberries**

115 g/4 oz icing sugar

meringue

2 tsp cornflour

300 g/10½ oz caster sugar

5 large egg whites

1 tsp cider vinegar

filling

**3 peaches, peeled, stoned
and chopped**

**250 g/9 oz fresh
raspberries**

**200 ml/7 fl oz crème
fraîche**

**150 ml/5 fl oz double
cream**

1 Preheat the oven to 150°C/300°F/Gas Mark 2. Brush a 35 x 25-cm/14 x 10-inch Swiss roll tin with oil and line with baking paper.

2 To make the coulis, process the raspberries and icing sugar to a purée. Press through a sieve into a bowl and set aside.

3 To make the meringue, sift the cornflour into a bowl and stir in the caster sugar. In a separate, spotlessly clean bowl, whisk the egg whites into stiff peaks, then whisk in the vinegar. Gradually whisk in the cornflour and sugar mixture until stiff and glossy.

4 Spread the meringue mixture evenly in the prepared tin, leaving a 1-cm/½-inch border. Bake in the centre of the preheated oven for 20 minutes, then reduce the heat to 110°C/225°F/Gas Mark ¼ and cook for a further 25–30 minutes, or until puffed up. Leave to cool for 15 minutes. Turn out onto another piece of baking paper and carefully remove the lining paper.

5 To make the filling, place the peaches in a bowl with the raspberries. Add 2 tablespoons of the coulis and mix. In a separate bowl, whisk the crème fraîche and cream together until thick. Spread over the meringue. Scatter the fruit over the cream, leaving a 3-cm/1¼-inch border at one short edge. Using the baking paper, lift and roll the meringue, starting at the short edge without the border, ending up seam-side down. Lift onto a plate and serve with the coulis.

profiteroles

SERVES 6

choux pastry

**70 g/2½ oz unsalted butter,
plus extra for greasing**

200 ml/7 fl oz water

100 g/3½ oz plain flour

3 eggs, beaten

cream filling

**300 ml/10 fl oz double
cream**

3 tbsp caster sugar

1 tsp vanilla extract

chocolate & brandy sauce

**125 g/4½ oz plain
chocolate, broken into
small pieces**

35 g/1¼ oz unsalted butter

6 tbsp water

2 tbsp brandy

1 Preheat the oven to 200°C/400°F/Gas Mark 6. Grease a large baking sheet.

2 To make the pastry, place the butter and water in a saucepan and bring to the boil. Meanwhile, sift the flour into a bowl. Turn off the heat and beat in the flour until smooth. Cool for 5 minutes. Beat in enough of the eggs to give the mixture a soft dropping consistency.

3 Transfer the pastry mixture to a piping bag fitted with a 1-cm/½-inch plain nozzle. Pipe small balls onto the prepared baking sheet. Bake in the preheated oven for 25 minutes. Pierce each ball with a skewer to let the steam escape.

4 To make the filling, whip the cream, sugar and vanilla extract together. Cut the pastry balls across the centre, then fill with cream.

5 To make the sauce, gently melt the chocolate, butter and water together in a small saucepan, stirring constantly, until smooth. Stir in the brandy. Pile the profiteroles into individual serving dishes, pour over the sauce and serve.

strawberry éclairs

MAKES ABOUT 18

choux pastry

**55 g/2 oz unsalted butter,
plus extra for greasing**

150 ml/5 fl oz water

8 tbsp plain flour

2 eggs, beaten

filling and topping

200 g/7 oz strawberries

2 tbsp icing sugar

**140 g/5 oz mascarpone
cheese**

1 Preheat the oven to 220°C/425°F/Gas Mark 7. Grease two baking sheets.

2 Heat the butter and water in a pan until boiling. Remove from the heat, quickly tip in the flour and beat until smooth. Gradually beat in the eggs with an electric hand-held whisk, until glossy. Spoon into a piping bag with a large plain nozzle and pipe eighteen 9-cm/3½-inch fingers on the baking sheets.

3 Bake in the preheated oven for 15–20 minutes until golden brown. Cut a slit down the side of each éclair to release steam. Bake for a further 2 minutes. Transfer to a wire rack to cool.

4 Purée half the strawberries with the icing sugar. Finely chop the remaining strawberries and stir into the mascarpone.

5 Pipe or spoon the mascarpone mixture into the éclairs. Serve the éclairs with the strawberry purée spooned over. Best served within an hour of filling.

almond & hazelnut gateau

SERVES 8

butter, for greasing

4 eggs

115 g/4 oz caster sugar

50 g/1¾ oz ground almonds

50 g/1¾ oz ground hazelnuts

50 g/1¾ oz plain flour

70 g/2½ oz flaked almonds

icing sugar, for dusting

filling

100 g/3½ oz plain chocolate, broken into pieces

1 tbsp butter

300 ml/10 fl oz double cream

1 Preheat the oven to 190°C/375°F/Gas Mark 5. Grease two 18-cm/7-inch sandwich tins and line with baking paper.

2 Whisk the eggs and caster sugar in a large mixing bowl with an electric hand-held whisk for about 10 minutes, or until the mixture is very light and foamy and a trail is left when the whisk is dragged across the surface. Fold in the ground nuts. Sift the flour and fold in with a metal spoon or palette knife. Divide the mixture between the prepared tins.

3 Scatter the flaked almonds over the top of one of the cakes. Bake both of the cakes in the preheated oven for 15–20 minutes, or until springy to the touch. Leave to cool slightly in the tins. Remove the cakes from the tins and transfer to a wire rack to cool completely. Meanwhile, make the filling. Melt the chocolate in a heatproof bowl set over a saucepan of gently simmering water, remove from the heat and stir in the butter. Leave the mixture to cool slightly. Whip the cream until just holding its shape, then fold in the melted chocolate mixture.

4 Place the cake without the extra almonds on a serving plate and spread the filling over it. Leave the filling to set slightly, then place the almond-topped cake on top and chill for about 1 hour. Dust with icing sugar and serve.

VARIATION

For a different type of nut topping, replace the flaked almonds with chopped walnuts.